The Landour Cookbook

I find a recipe is much like a... play, which...
... a play, and have fun with a
variation.

...Madhur Beauti

I feel a recipe is only a theme, which an intelligent cook can play each time with a variation.

Madam Benoit

The Landour Cookbook

Over Hundred Years Of Hillside Cooking

Edited And Introduced By

RUSKIN BOND

&

GANESH SAILI

Lustre Press
Roli Books

978-81-7436-163-9

First published in 2001
This edition published in 2014
Third impression 2017

Roli Books Pvt. Ltd.,
Lustre Press
M-75, Greater Kailash II (Market)
New Delhi 110 048, India
Ph: ++91 (011) 4068 2000
E-mail: info@rolibooks.com
Website: www.rolibooks.com

Cover Design: Shrabani Desgupta

Printed at Nutech Print Services, New Delhi.

Contents

The Landour Cookbook is chock-a-block with recipes that were often experiments by countless men and women whose experiences in the kitchen have been recorded faithfully. So try them out in the same spirit.

There is a variety of measurements used. (We have added equivalent modern measurements alongside.)

1 pint (pt)	568 ml
1 lt (litre)	1.76 pt
1 oz (ounce)	28.35 gm
1 lb (pound)	453.6 gm
1 kg (kilogram)	2.2 lb
1 qt (quart)	1.1 lt or 2 pt
1 gill	142 ml
1 gallon (gal)	4.55 lt
1 seer	1 kg or 1 lt
pao	250 gm
chattack	62.5 gm

Oven Temperatures

°Fahrenheit	*°Celsius*
250°F	130°C
300°F	150°C
350°F	180°C
400°F	200°C

Introduction

Ruskin's Granny had a collection of kitchen proverbs that she used from time to time. Her culinary efforts were fairly simple as was the case in most Anglo-Indian or domiciled European households in India. Nothing very fancy. The recipes of *The Landour Cookbook* are in a way different from the general diet of the average resident of the hill station. There is a distinct American flavour to them.

Landour was the headquarters of the American missionary community in India, for about 100 years (1850 to 1950). They enjoyed a standard of living that was even more affluent than that of the British official families. They certainly did not undergo any culinary hardships, as any student of these recipes will realise, whether they were on furlough in Mussoorie or spreading the 'good word' in the far corners of the subcontinent.

Bond in his childhood grew up on curry and rice for lunch and, probably, Roast Lamb for dinner and this diet did not vary very much except on special occasions. In fact, his grandmother would admonish him for asking for a second helping with her favourite proverb: 'Don't let your tongue cut your throat!' Now years later Ruskin Bond is making up for those frugal boyhood years by wading into dishes described in this book, provided someone is willing to make them. Gentle reader, if any of you have gone to the trouble of preparing Kofta Korma or Tamale Pie please do send portions of your efforts to Mr. Saili and Mr. Bond for proper evaluation.

The tradition of exotic cooking continues on the hillside, long after the missionaries have departed, in the culinary efforts of Lakshmi Tripathi's Chicken in Garlic Sauce, Victor and Maya Banerjee's Burmese Kaukswe, Nandu Jauhar's Chicken in White Sauce, Pramod and Kiran Kapoor's outdoors *dum pukth* style . . . (however, we cannot include these recipes due to space constraints).

The local milkmen still have a tradition of watering their milk. Ruskin Bond's milk gets watered at Victor Banerjee's water tap, much to Victor's glee. Little does Victor know that his own milk gets watered at Pramod Kapoor's tap – much to Pramod's glee!

Nevertheless, we are grateful to the *doodhwalas* for being an ever-present help in times of trouble. For example, during Prohibition (in Morarji's rule!) the milkmen would bring us their country-made brew in our hot-water bottles. The trouble was that our beds would stink of *kachi*, forcing us to throw out our bottles on cold winter nights. For more than a century, the milkmen have been plodding up and down the mountain, providing Landour and Mussoorie with milk of various textures, and without their contribution half these dishes would not have been possible.

Among the other services provided by the milkmen are fresh mountain trout from the Algar River. These are appreciated on the hillside as fresh fish is not always available. They are rather small and bony, but very tasty; and as Ruskin's Granny used to say: 'Better a small fish than an empty dish!'

John Copeman (though no missionary!) built a Garhwali-style house and settled down in the nearby village of Patrani for some time. He knew how to get through a bottle in one sitting and follow it up with Roast Chicken.

Another very popular variation of this dish is often served to Nandu Jauhar's personal guests at the Savoy Hotel. We must remember that his cook, Sher Singh, used to once work for the missionaries and has saved up his Chicken in White Sauce recipe for Nandu's personal use.

You'll notice how the one common thing in every other recipe is the humble potato. And thereby hangs a tale. 'Seeds of the potato-berries should be sown in adapted places by explorers of new countries.' So wrote a botanical-minded empire-builder. Among the many officials who took this advice were Captain Young of the Sirmur Rifles and Mr. Shore, Superintendent of the Doon. Captain Young may have had personal reasons for carrying out the directive. He was an Irishman and liked potatoes.

While he was deliberating where to sow his potatoes, some men from Garhwal arrived and mentioned that they too were fond of the new Irish potatoes and had tried growing them in the hills with some success. They suggested that the Captain should try the upper part of the range directly in front of the Doon.

Captain Young and Mr. Shore set out on foot and soon left the sub-tropical forest behind them. Above 4,000 feet they came to the oak and rhododendron forests, and above 6,000 feet they found the deodars. The climate was so cool and delightful that they forgot all about putting down potatoes and, instead, erected a small hunting-lodge on the northern slopes of the mountain.

Apart from the inhabitants of a few scattered villages, no one lived on the upper slopes of the mountain. Bears, leopards, and barking-deer roamed the forest. There were pheasants in the shady ravines and Himalayan trout in the Algar River to the north. Two years later, Captain Young, who had by this time become a Colonel, built the first house of the settlement. It was called Mullingar, after his home in Ireland, and it can still be seen on the way up to what became Landour Cantonment. Then, on a spur of the same hill, he built Annfield, but this is now a ruin. Other people began to follow Colonel Young's example, and by 1830 the twin hill stations of Landour and Mussoorie had come into being.

A suitable name for the new station might have been Mount Aloo; but Mussoorie got is name from the Mansur berry (*coriara nepalenis*) – a shrub that grows abundantly in the area but has little use. Mansuri, therefore, ought to be the correct name and spelling, but the British never could get local names right.

In the old days, the Landour bakers were a common sight on the road, with their trunks on their heads selling their breads and confectionery. As Granny would say: 'Dry bread at home is better than Roast Lamb abroad.'

But one of the bakers felt that life would be much better abroad. He was so popular with the young ladies on the hillside that one of them decided to marry him and take him off to America. From running the Sunshine Bakery in Landour, he went up in life and was last heard as the Bun King of Montana. Today, most of them end up in Dubai. But their original home is in Ghoghas, a little village 40 miles from Tehri, from where their ancestors came with the refugee prince, Suleman Shikoh in the summer of 1658.

Among the many things that the old bakers made were fudge, stick jaw, marzipan and meringues, which some of us remember from our childhood. These have been passed on and perhaps, today's fast foods may have accounted for the demise of many of these home-made snacks from the 1930s and 40s.

Though in its heyday, the late-lamented Savoy Bakery was famed for its Scones and Currant Teacakes. And a little way down the Charleville road was that great eatery, the Riviera, famous for its soups. It is said that on a bad day, you knew the soup was not hot enough if the waiter could keep his thumb in it. We stand convinced by some of the old timers on the hillside that the following customer-waiter exchanges were born there:

Waiter, there's a fly in my soup.
That must be a very small chicken, sir.

Waiter, there's a dead fly in my soup.
Yes, sir, it's the heat that kills them.

Waiter, there's a fly in my soup.
They don't care what they eat, do they, sir?

Waiter, there's a fly in my soup.
Don't make a fuss, sir. They'll all want one.

Waiter, what's this fly doing in my soup?
Looks like the breaststroke to me, sir.

*Waiter, I can't find any chicken in the Chicken
Soup!*
Well, you won't find any horse in the horseradish
either!

Waiter, there's a fly in my ice cream!
It's come for winter sports, sir!

* * * *

We must remember that these recipes were enjoyed
only by the fortunate few. World War II was in
progress and there was food rationing in India and
sometimes there was drought and famine in parts of
the country. However, we do not wish to deviate from
the culinary skill that went into the making of these
unusual dishes. They are as delicious today as they
were 60 years ago, and are well worth the effort that's
put into recreating them. A pity there are no survivors
from that period otherwise we'd have been able to
meet and talk to them. However, some of these old
khansamas survive. It was to these professionals that
the housewives of the Landour Community turned,
in order, to make these imaginative recipes a reality.
Among the survivors from that period who are still
around are Makhan Lal, the Hackney's cook who ran
the Redburn Guest House till it was sold and Sher
Singh, who used to work for the Skillmans at Tafton.
No one would say that he's a bad cook – but one does

wonder whether his Apple Pie is really supposed to glow in the dark! Kundan Singh was the Alter's cook at Oakville till they went to America and he retired to Mullingar with his family. His Banana Fritters are a smashing hit. Occasionally, you'll find him at work in Ganesh's place, where he treats the guests like gods... by putting burnt offerings before them!

Among the many local cooks who worked for the missionaries was Ranjit, an eccentric character who spoke his mind on everything under the sun. At one time he worked for a Bishop of the Hindustani Church, who was given to criticising his guests behind their backs. When the Bishop threw a big dinner party in Landour, Ranjit had made up his mind to quit his job. As the entourage entered the dining room, they found Ranjit comfortably ensconced at the head of the table.

'Out! out!' yelled the Bishop, pointing to the door.

'You out! Out yourself!' replied Ranjit calmly, and proceeded to tell the guests what their genial host actually thought of them!

* * * *

Most of the missionary children went to Woodstock. Most of the young men and women had healthy appetites, which had to be satisfied when they came home hence the inventiveness of these recipes. So well nourished were the Woodstock boys and girls that in the Mussoorie Olympics they outran the underfed orphans of Wynberg-Allen or the students of Oakgrove, the Railway School in Jharipani, who were fed on a frugal diet which strictly followed the Keventer's Railway Menu. The annual May Sale, then and now, remains the testing ground for these recipes. People would make confectionery to be sold at the various food stalls. In the same way, this tradition continues. But today you're likely to get Tibetan, Korean or north-eastern cuisine, which reflect the different ethnic backgrounds of the student body and teaching staff.

Recalls our friend Norman Van Rooy, an old Woodstock alumnus, born to missionary parents, who lived in Redburn Cottage in the 1970s, the Pulling Taffy concocted by their cook: 'The pulling taffy lived up to its name, if you weren't pulling it, you were using it for whacking each other on the head!'

Although Landour was basically a missionary headquarters, nevertheless, it had other residents who let their hair down occasionally and were not averse to a little romance or wenching. The fun seeking ones had an ally in the then stationmaster who, whenever the young men debouched at the Dehra Railway Station, would direct them to the lonely grass widows on the hillside. Often an absent husband turned up without warning and there was hell to pay.

The Mussoorie Miscellany of 1936 tells us of one such incident: 'On July 25, 1927, at the height of the season, in the heart of the town, and in broad daylight, there occurred a double tragedy that certainly set the station agog. It happened in a full boarding house and thus provided more than a season's "thrill" for the residents, and had, too, its comic elements.

'Soon after midday the boarders were startled into expectancy and brisk activity when a shot rang out from one of the rooms and a woman screamed. Other shots followed in quick succession. Those unfortunate boarders who happened to be in the public rooms, verandas, or outside, dived for safety of their own apartments and bolted the doors as soon as they were aware of what was happening. One unhappy boarder, however, ignorant of where the desperate man with the gun might be at the moment, came around the corner with his arms well above his head taking no chances of being mistaken for one of the shooter's captors – for captors were manoeuvring by then to lay the destroyer – and, as luck would have it, ran straight into the levelled pistol. And even the man who held it and had just killed his own wife, laughed!'

You might laugh too, but, say what you will, it was a delicate situation to face and a wise precaution which the gentleman took, for even the armed police had to tread warily when they arrived. 'Mr. O, who carried the weapon, shot his wife dead, wounded his daughter and finally, shot himself. His was, perhaps, the only

Christian cremation in Mussoorie, performed in compliance with his own wishes expressed long before his unfortunate end.'

Subsequently, some of the Landour boarding houses followed the example of the Savoy and Charleville Hotels and introduced a separation-bell, which was rung at four in the morning to warn adulterers to get back to their rooms before they were discovered by irate husbands and wives in flagrante delicto. A naughty place Mussoorie was in the good old days! Does such entertainment still exist on our quiet hillside?

Along with the cooks, some of the old houses have survived. The unique bylaws of Landour Cantonment permitted no building except for a few government ones. So, the houses are almost exactly as they were over a 100 years ago: the New Zealand mission called theirs by the Maori name Ate-o-roa or the Long White Cloud while the Hawaiians preferred Aloha. Ellangowan and Chennyowyth (good Welsh names) still house the Mennonites.

Most of the old residents have long since departed, but their old houses are still in use. There are some lovely old houses in the Landour Cantonment but, sadly, the majority of them lie empty for most of the year. Their owners, the famous and the wealthy, live elsewhere and visit Mussoorie or Landour about once a year, for a weekend's relaxation. It's everyone's dream to own a house in Landour. But once a property has been bought and done up nicely, it's usually forgotten.

A different situation prevails in the 'civil' station of Mussoorie. There we have an acute shortage of accommodation for local residents, not helped by a complete ban on any sort of building, be it hostel or private residence. As a result, the economy is stagnating. In Landour, there is no economy to speak off. The only substantial bank depositors are the handful of NGOs (non-governmental organisations) and inland missions who operate from this area.

From November to March you can take a walk up to Lal Tibba or around the Landour *chakkar* without meeting a soul except for a milkman, whose home is down in the valley, or a *chowkidar* from one of the empty houses, or maybe, if you're lucky, Professor Uniyal the only year-round resident at the top of the hill. More often than not, he's enjoying the privacy of his garden, tending his wayward nasturtiums and antirrhinums. One wanders on, past Victor Banerjee's pretty gingerbread house, Prannoy Roy's eyrie, Tom Alter's rambling family estate, and the stately homes owned by the absent Lals, Kapoors, Misras, and others, in the hope of stumbling upon some intellectual company. But alas, there is no one in residence – all, all are gone, the old familiar faces! If you're lucky, you might get a glimpse of them next summer, but even that is doubtful.

Where are our distinguished travel writers? The Gantzers are in Singapore, encouraging tourism there. Bill Aitken has gone south and will return only when the wild ducks fly north; his contribution to Mussoorie's cuisine consists of Scottish Porridge. As Granny used to say: 'There is skill in all things even in making porridge.'

Ah! Here's Brigadier Yadav – always good for a tale or two of his days as ADC (aide-de-camp) to Mountbatten. His enthusiasm never flags. But the good Brigadier looks gloomy today. 'I've had enough of this place,' he complains. 'Not a soul to talk to. And I can't take the cold any more – thinking of moving down to Rajpur.'

One more empty house!

There's one last hope of finding a little company – the cemetery! Those rows of old, weather-worn graves tell of livelier times, when officers and gentlemen tossed back their rum punches and whiskey pegs, no doubt hastening their journey to this final abode. But, confounded luck, the cemetery gate is locked and chained, barred to prowlers like me. Now even converse with the dead is denied.

Never mind, there's always Lakshmi's *chowkidar*. Not much by way of intellectual stimulation, but the hooch isn't bad. He may not be encouraging tourism, but at least he helps the local get through the lean days.

In the old days, Mackinnon and Bohle helped thirsty locals quench their parched throats by starting breweries which were successful for a few years. The final big push in the brewing business, began in 1876 with the advent of Whimper and Company who leased the 'Crown Brewery'. Men declare that the mother of invention is necessity; in Mussoorie's beery business, however, Accident ousted Necessity, put a new component into the formula, and brewed more beer – and a little trouble. Unexpectedly, everyone suddenly acclaimed a much improved brew and the source was traced to Vat 42, whereon everyone re-drank, re-tasted, and re-tested, till the diminishing beer uncovered the delightfully brewed remains of a tourist! Poor fellow, he had fallen in unnoticed, been drowned, and all unknown to himself, had given the beer trade a real fillip. Meat was, thereafter, recognised as the missing component and was scrupulously added till more modern, and less cannibalistic, means were discovered to satiate the froth blower.

Come to think of it, Granny always had it right:

'Eating and drinking shouldn't keep men from thinking.'

Beverages

CRANBERRY

Marsh-covered tracts of wind-swept wilderness,
Vast wastes, the haunt of coot and flamingo;
And ghostly shadows over all, where man
Had lost his heritage until I came
And covered o'er those bogs with vine and fruit.
And now behold! That wilderness erstwhile
So bare and useless to the human race,
Has filled man's purse with gold, and given him
Good cheer and colour bright for his holiday.

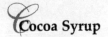

Cocoa Syrup

Mrs. A. B. Harper

½ cup sugar
½ cup cocoa
½ tsp salt
2 cups cold water

Mix sugar, cocoa, salt and cold water thoroughly. Stir till well blended. Cook slowly for 15 to 20 minutes, till the syrup is thick.

Use 1 to 2 tsp of this syrup to each cup of milk in making cocoa for children.

Prepare in quantities and store in bottles. Children love this drink.

—◆—

Cocoa Syrup

E. L. Moody

2 cups water
2 cups sugar
1 cup cocoa
½ tsp salt
½ tsp vanilla

Mix all the ingredients and boil for about 10 minutes. Use 3 tbsp to a large glass of milk and stir well. Children like it.

—◆—

Lemon Syrup

12 cups water
2 cups lemon juice
12 cups sugar

Combine all the ingredients and let it boil for 3 minutes. Store the syrup in bottles. This will keep for several months.

Lime Juice Syrup

1 seer lime juice, strained
1 seer white sugar
½ lb lime rind, thinly cut

Dissolve the sugar in the lime juice, and while boiling, skim until it becomes clear. Add the rind and simmer for about 5 minutes. Then strain through a jelly bag and pour while hot into bottles corking at once. To every quart of syrup, add 1 tsp brandy when bottled. This has been tried and can be stored for two hot seasons.

Ginger Beer   Mrs. Caldwell

Pour boiling water over 1 heaped tbsp ground ginger. Strain through a sieve or thin cloth and add 1 tsp citric acid, 1 cup sugar and ½ tsp soda. Mix well. Add water to taste.

Ginger Syrup

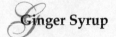

Mrs. F. C. Martin

1 seer sugar
¾ seer boiling water

Stir till the sugar dissolves completely. Add 1 tbsp citric acid dissolved in a little hot water. When cool, strain and add 1 tbsp ginger beer essence.

Ginger Ale Punch

Mrs. L. B. Rambo

4 lemons
2 cups sugar
4 or 5 stalks mint
2 bottles ginger ale

Chop the lemons into thin slices and keep in a large bowl. Add the sugar and mint and pour 1 qt boiling water. Let the mixture stand till cold. Add ice and ginger ale just before serving.

Nectar Cream

Mrs. Nugent

6 lb sugar
4 oz tartaric acid
2 qt water

Mix all the ingredients and boil for ½ an hour and then strain. When warm, add 4 stiffly-beaten egg whites. Add 1 tbsp lemon acid. Store in bottles and use in a glass of water. It is a cooling drink.

Fruit Punch   E. L. Moody

4 cups sugar
8 cups water
1 can pineapple, grated
1 cup fruit juice
1 qt strawberries, cut in slices
4 bananas, sliced
6 oranges, juice
3 lemon cups (3 or 4 oranges if desired)
1 tin cherries

Boil the sugar and water for 5 minutes. Cool and add the remaining ingredients. Serves about 25 people.

 **Mint Sherbet**   Mrs. Riddle

Take a small bunch of mint and bruise the leaves. Add the juice of 2 lemons, and keep this covered for 10 or 15 minutes. Meanwhile, dissolve 2 cups sugar in 2 cups water and boil without stirring till a fine thread spins. Remove from the fire, add the mint leaves flavoured with lemon juice and ½ cup orange juice. Cool and strain.

Cranberry Drink

1 qt cranberries
2 lemons
2 oranges
2½ cups sugar
1 stick cinnamon
12 cloves

Grind all the fruits together. Add 1 cup water and boil for 5 minutes. Strain the mixture and add the sugar. While still hot, add cinnamon and cloves. Cool and when ready to serve, add water to taste.

❦

Coffee

10 tbsp coffee powder
1 egg
30 cups hot water

Moisten the coffee powder with the egg. Add a little warm water, if necessary. Add water and boil the mixture for a few minutes.

❦

Hot Spiced Tea

1 tsp cinnamon, ground
1 tsp cloves, ground
2 cups sugar
6 qt boiling water
3 tbsp tea
1½ cups orange juice
¾ cup lemon juice

Tie the cinnamon and cloves in a cloth bag. Add this spice bag and sugar to boiling water and boil together for 5 minutes. Remove from the heat. Then tie the tea in a loose cloth and add to the sugar syrup. Cover and let this stand for 5 minutes. Remove the spice and the tea bag. Now add the juices. Serve hot.

Soups

❧

'Tis very plain for all to see
The first place, falls easily to me
On the Menu Card alone I stand,
And S-O-U-P looks quite grand
"An old time friend" the hungry say,
And order a dish up straight away.
The rich man smiles to find me hot
And tips the waiter for what he has brought.
The poor man sits and sips his fill
And straight away gladly pays his bill.
The cook can easily get me up
From an old spare bone or leftover cup
'Tis a piece of meat or a vegetable stew
Most anything for soups will do.

Myrtle Furman

Cream of Vegetable Soup

Mrs. A. B. Harper

2 cups milk
3 tsp butter
4 tsp flour
salt
1 cup cooked, seasoned and
sifted vegetables such as spinach,
carrot, peas, beans, and corn

Heat the milk over a double boiler. Melt the butter in a pan. Stir in the flour till smooth. Add the milk slowly. Add the salt and bring the mixture to a boil. Remove from the fire at once. Heat the vegetables while the soup is cooking and blend them together.

Vegetable Soup

2 carrots, ground
1 onion, ground
¼ head cabbage, ground
2 turnips, ground
2 okra, sliced
4 tomatoes, sliced
½ cup green beans, chopped
celery chopped
(and any other vegetable in season)
2 potatoes, finely chopped
2½ cups water
2½ cups meat stock
salt
pepper

Combine all the vegetables (except the potatoes) and boil in 2½ cups water until nearly done. Add the potatoes and boil until all the vegetables are tender. Add the meat stock, salt and pepper to taste. Cook for ½ an hour more. Serve hot.

❦

Peanut Butter Soup
M. M. Saum

1 pt milk
1 onion, sliced
4 tbsp peanut butter
2 tbsp flour
2 cups vegetable stock
1 tsp salt
a pinch of pepper

Scald the milk with the onion. Mix the peanut butter with flour and when well blended add to the scalded milk mixture. Stir until the milk mixture is thick and very smooth. Pour this mixture in a double boiler. Cover and cook for 15 minutes. Before serving, add the vegetable stock. Check for seasoning.

Note: The onion may be omitted and the milk substituted for vegetable stock.

❦

Cheese Soup
Hiram Ohio Cookbook

1 qt milk
1 tbsp onion, sliced
1 blade mace
2 tbsp butter
2 tbsp flour

½ cup cheese, grated
1 tsp salt
¼ tsp white pepper powder
2 egg yolks, beaten

Scald the milk, onion and mace. Melt the butter and mix in the flour. Strain the milk and add gradually to the butter mixture. When creamy, add the cheese, salt and white pepper powder, stirring till the cheese has melted. Then add the beaten egg yolks. Whip the mixture with an egg beater till frothy. Serve immediately.

Tomato Soup

1 can tomatoes
1 pt water
12 black peppercorns
bit of bay leaf
4 cloves
1 onion, sliced
1 tsp sugar
1 tsp salt
$1/_3$ tsp soda
2 tbsp butter
3 tbsp flour

Cook the tomatoes, water, black peppercorns, bay leaf, cloves, onion and sugar for 20 minutes. When the tomatoes turn soft, strain the mixture and add the salt and soda. In a pan, melt the butter; add the flour browning it slightly. Now add the tomato mixture and stir well till it becomes slightly thick. Serve hot.

Cream of Tomato Soup

1 qt tomatoes
salt and pepper to taste
1 pt milk
¼ tsp soda
1 tbsp butter

Boil the tomatoes, strain and heat the juice till very hot. Add the salt and pepper to taste. Heat the milk in another pan. Mix in the soda and butter. Then quickly pour the tomato juice into the milk. Serve.

Cream of Potato Soup

4 potatoes
1 onion, chopped
1 qt milk
½ tsp salt
pepper to taste
1 tbsp butter

Boil the potatoes and onion in a little water until done. Mash the vegetables and then pour in the milk. Add the salt, pepper to taste and butter. Mix well. Serve hot.

Salmon Soup

2 qt milk
2 tbsp flour
2 tbsp butter

1 tin salmon
1 tsp salt
pepper to taste

Heat the milk to boil point. Mix the flour in a little cold milk till smooth. Add this to the hot milk. Let it boil. Add the butter, salmon, salt and pepper. Mix well.

Serve hot with crackers or toast.

————❦————

Egg and Milk Soup

Mrs. Bauman

2 cups scalded milk
2 eggs, slightly beaten
$1/_8$ tsp salt
a pinch of pepper

Add the eggs to the scalded milk, stirring constantly until the mixture thickens slightly. Add the salt and pepper. Do not boil the mixture. Serve at once.

It is very nutritious and easily digested. This recipe can be changed easily into a dessert by substituting 2 tbsp sugar for salt and pepper.

Entree and Tiffin Dishes

❦

THE TOMATO

I am the apple of love
As bright as the setting sun.
At home I rhyme with potato,
But here it can never be done,
Mine is an evil family,
But I've lived the stigma down.
And though I am still a night shade,
I'm eaten from my heart to my gown.

Dr. G. E. Miller

Potato Soufflé

1 egg, separated
1 cup potato, mashed
1 tbsp cream
salt and pepper to taste

Beat the egg yolk and add to the potato with cream and seasoning. Beat till the mixture is smooth and light. Add the beaten egg white. Pour the mixture into a greased baking dish and bake till brown.

Cheese Soufflé
Hiram Ohio Cookbook

1 cup milk
1 tbsp butter
3 tbsp flour
2 eggs, separated
1 cup cheese
½ tsp salt

Heat the milk and butter. Mix the flour with a little milk and add to the milk mixture. Cook thoroughly. Beat in the egg yolks and cheese. Remove the mixture from the fire and fold in the egg whites. Bake for 20 minutes. Serve at once.

Spinach Soufflé

6 tbsp spinach, chopped, cooked
2 cups cream (or milk)
2 tbsp flour

1 tbsp butter
½ tsp salt
a pinch of pepper
1 egg, separated

Make a creamy sauce of milk, flour and butter. Add the salt and pepper. Beat the egg yolk and mix in the spinach. Add this to the sauce mixture. Remove from the fire. When fairly cool, fold in the beaten egg white. Bake in buttered ramekins.

<hr>

Eggs in Nests (Serves: 6)

Mrs. A. B. Harper

1 cup milk
1 tbsp flour
1 tbsp butter
½ tsp salt and pepper
leftover minced chicken
6 slices of buttered toast
6 eggs, separated

Make a cream sauce of milk, flour, butter, salt and pepper and add the minced chicken. Place the slices of buttered toast in a baking dish. Spread the creamed chicken on each toast. Take one egg for each slice of toast, separate the yolks and whites. Beat the whites until very stiff and arrange on top of the creamed chicken in circular forms like a bird's nest. Place a whole raw yolk in each nest. Bake just long enough to set the yolk and slightly brown the whites. Serve hot.

<hr>

Cheese Fondue

1 cup breadcrumbs
1 cup cheese, grated
1 cup sweet milk
3 tbsp melted butter
1 tsp salt
1 tsp red pepper
3 eggs, separated, beaten

Combine all the ingredients and mix well. Bake in an oven till brown.

❧

Spanish Rice (Serves: 6)

¼ cup white rice
1½ cups onions, sliced
4 tbsp green pepper, diced
3 whole cloves
3 tbsp fat
1 bay leaf
3½ cups tomatoes, cooked
3 tsp granulated sugar
1¾ tsp salt

Cook the rice until tender. Meanwhile, cook the sliced onions in the fat until soft. Add the remaining ingredients and simmer for 15 minutes. Remove the bay leaf and cloves, and add the rice. Turn the rice mixture into a greased baking casserole dish, and bake in a moderately hot oven (375°F) for 30 minutes.

❧

Peanut Rice
Mrs. E. Livengood

1 cup boiled rice (hot)
½ cup peanuts, chopped, roasted
½ cup breadcrumbs
1 egg
a little milk

Mix all the ingredients and moisten with a little milk. Bake in a buttered tin for about ½ an hour. Serve with brown sauce or tomato sauce. Cheese sauce can also be used.

Rice and Tomato

2 cups rice
2 cups strained tomato pulp
2 onions, browned
½ lb bacon, fried

Cook the rice in water to which has been added strained tomato. Drain. Place on a platter and top with browned onion and fried bacon. The onion can be fried in bacon fat. Serve with lettuce salad.

Rice Mould with Cheese Sauce
Mrs. H. E. Wylie

1 cup rice
3 tbsp butter
½ cup cream
2 egg yolks
2 tbsp butter

3 tbsp flour
½ tsp salt
2 cups milk
½ cup cheese

Boil the rice till done. While hot, mix a little butter, cream and beaten egg yolks. Pour the mixture in a mould and bake in a pan of boiling water in a moderate oven at 350°F till firm.
For the cheese sauce, cook the butter, flour and salt together till frothy. Add the milk slowly and stir till thick. Lastly add the cheese and serve warm.

———

Sopa Aros (A Mexican Rice Dish)

1 cup rice
1 tbsp shortening
1 medium-sized onion
1 cup fresh or tinned tomatoes
3 cups boiling water
salt, paprika or cayenne pepper
1 cup minced meat

Wash and thoroughly dry the rice. Cracked rice is best for this dish. When the fat is piping hot, brown the sliced onion, then add the rice, stirring carefully so as not to burn it. Add the tomatoes. Gradually, add the boiling water. Add the meat last. Cook gently for an hour or more. Reheat and serve. Any bits of cold roast, steak or ham will do.

———

Rice a la Peru

M. Manry

2 cups rice
1 onion, finely chopped
½ cup fat
3 cups boiling water
salt

Pour the fat over the onion in a large saucepan. Cook until the onion is translucent. Add the boiling water and bring the mixture to a boil. Add the well-washed rice to the boiling mixture. Let it boil gently for some time. When the water is nearly evaporated, add the salt and lower the heat. Let the mixture simmer until done.

❧

Spanish Rice

Mrs. P. A. Friesen

1 onion, finely chopped
1 slice bacon, chopped
4 medium-sized tomatoes
1 cup cold, boiled rice
salt and pepper

Cook the bacon and onion in a frying pan till brown. Add the tomatoes, then the rice. Season to taste with salt and pepper.

❧

Spaghetti, Italian Style

6 tbsp olive oil
3 or 4 onions, sliced
2 cloves garlic

1 can tomatoes
1 lb spaghetti, boiled in salt water, drained
salt and pepper

Heat the oil in a pan. Add the onions and garlic. When tender, add the tomatoes and let the mixture simmer for 45 minutes. Then press through a strainer and add the spaghetti. Mix well and dot with butter.

Spanish Spaghetti

2 slices of bacon
3 tbsp olive oil or lard
1 onion, sliced
3 cups dry spaghetti
1½ cups boiling water
1 can tomatoes
2 tsp salt
2 tsp sugar
a pinch of soda
2 or 3 red peppers
½ cup cheese, grated

Fry the bacon in oil. Add the onion. When really hot, add the spaghetti. Fry slowly, stirring constantly. When the mixture turns a rich brown, pour in boiling water, tomatoes, salt, sugar, soda and red peppers. Simmer slowly for 40 or 50 minutes. Keep covered, but do not let the mixture become dry. Add more boiling water, if required. Sprinkle grated cheese on top and keep in the oven before serving.

Chipino

2 large onions, chopped
1 green pepper, chopped
a pinch of parsley
a small clove of garlic
1 large chicken or 2 small ones
(duck or other meat may be used)
3 tbsp olive oil
1 can tomatoes
a handful of mushrooms
a handful of olives
salt and pepper

Cook the oil and chicken in a large pan. After a few minutes, add the vegetables and cook for 1 hour, stirring frequently. Cook till tender. Then add the tomatoes and a handful of mushrooms. After stewing for a few minutes, add a handful of olives. Boil for a few minutes more, then add the salt and pepper. Serve hot.

Luncheon Dish

½ cup butter
3 medium-sized onions
1 lb steak
1 can tomatoes
1 packet spaghetti, boiled in salt water, drained
salt and pepper

Melt the butter and fry the onions. Fry the steak after removing the onions. Cook till nearly tender. Add the tomatoes and bring the mixture to a boil. Add the spaghetti and mix well. Season to taste.

Liver Luncheon Dish

1 lb or less of liver
2 cups rice
1 tsp salt
½ lb or less of bacon
1 tbsp butter
1 onion
2 tbsp flour

Boil the rice in water with salt. When cooked, drain and turn on a platter. Having boiled the liver in salt water, grate or grind it and sprinkle it over the rice. Then fry the bacon and place it on the platter.

For the gravy, fry the chopped onion in the butter. Add the flour and fry till brown. Stir in some of the liver water and part milk if desired. Salad may be served with this.

———

Sweet Potato Surprise   Mrs. P. A. Friesen

This dish taste delicious with fried chicken or cold meat for luncheon. You can fry them any time and reheat them in the oven at mealtime or even the next day. They will taste the same as when freshly cooked.

2 cups sweet potatoes
1 egg, beaten
½ tsp salt
dash of pepper
½ cup crushed cornflakes or bran flakes
marshmallows, if obtainable

Boil and peel the potatoes, put through a grater. When partly cool, add the egg, salt and pepper. If the mixture is too dry, add a little milk. Flour hands, if necessary, and make 8 round balls from the mixture with marshmallow hidden inside. Roll the balls in cornflakes or bran flakes. Fry in hot fat till brown and drain on soft absorbent paper.

Scalloped Onions or Cabbage and Peanuts

6 onions
2 tbsp flour
1 cup milk
1 tsp salt
½ cups peanuts, chopped
½ cup breadcrumbs

Cook the onions in boiling, salt water till soft. Make a white sauce with a little butter, flour, milk and salt. Add the onions and peanuts and mix. Pour this mixture in a buttered baking dish. Cover with breadcrumbs. Dot with bits of butter. Bake till brown.

Stuffed Dal

boiled dal (moist)
salt and pepper
2 or 3 slices of stale bread
1 potato
1 onion
mixed herbs
a little butter

Add some salt and pepper to the boiled dal. Put a layer of the dal in the bottom of a buttered baking dish, (the dal layer should be 1½" deep). Then add a layer of stuffing made of ground bread, potato and onion mixed with herbs, salt, pepper and a little butter. Add another layer of dal on top. Dot with bits of butter. Bake in a slow oven until the potatoes in the stuffing are completely tender.

———❧———

Goulash

2 onions
2 tbsp fat
1 tsp paprika
2 tsp salt
2 lb thick round steak, diced
6 potatoes, diced
hot water
1 cup tomatoes

Fry the onions in the fat for 1 minute. Add the paprika, salt and steak. Stir well. Stew for 1 hour, adding a little hot water, occasionally, to prevent the mixture from burning. Before the meat is tender (20 minutes before serving) add the potatoes and tomatoes. Cover with boiling water. When the vegetables are tender, serve. Keep a tight lid on the saucepan.

Chop Suey (Serves: 10)   M. R. Long

½ lb steak, diced
2 tbsp fat
1 bunch celery, finely cut
4 onions, finely cut
3 cups stewed or fresh tomatoes

salt

$1/_8$ tsp cayenne pepper

1 tbsp butter

1 tin red kidney beans

Cook the meat in fat for 3 minutes. Add the celery and onions. Simmer for 10 minutes. Add the tomatoes, salt, cayenne pepper and butter. Simmer till tender. Add the kidney beans. Cook for 4 minutes. Serve with boiled rice.

Omelette

M. M. Saum

6 eggs, beaten separately

½ pt milk

6 tsp cornstarch

1 tsp baking powder

a little salt

Combine all the ingredients together and lastly, add the beaten egg whites. If desired, add minced ham or chicken just before cooking. Cook in a hot skillet with butter or clarified butter.

Baked Eggs

1. Butter a baking dish, and break in the eggs. Add 2 tbsp milk, seasoning and cheese, if desired. Bake in the oven for a few minutes.

2. Grind leftover meat and line it in the bottom of a baking dish. Break the eggs on top, Add a few tbsp of butter, salt and pepper to taste and a little milk, mix and bake.

3. Line a baking dish with leftover rice. Add a little tomato juice and break in the eggs. Add the salt, pepper and bits of butter. Mix and bake.

Servings on Toast

1. Mix the hard-boiled sliced eggs with the cream sauce (see Spinach Souffle for cream sauce recipe). Add the salt, pepper and paprika. Mix well and serve on toast.

2. *Tomato Cream Toast*

> 1½ cups tomato, strained
> ¼ tsp soda
> 3 tbsp butter
> 3 tbsp flour
> ½ cup scalded milk
> ½ tsp salt

Melt the butter, add the flour and mix well. Stir in the tomato mixed with soda. Add the scalded milk and salt, mix well. Serve on toast.

3. *Welsh Rarebit*

> 1 cup cheese, grated
> 1 tbsp butter
> ½ pt milk
> 1 egg, beaten

Melt the cheese and butter in a pan over a gentle heat. Pour in the milk and egg, and cook. Serve on toast.

Mexican Rarebit

2 cups tomatoes, stewed
a little bit of butter
salt to taste
red pepper
1 cup mild cheese
3 eggs, separated

Heat the stewed tomatoes. Add the butter, salt, red pepper and cheese cut into small pieces. When the cheese melts, add the well-beaten yolks. When the mixture thickens, fold in the stiffly-beaten egg whites.

Serve hot on crackers or toast.

Corn Delight

2 cups potatoes
1 cup corn
½ cup onion, chopped
1 slice bacon
4 cups milk
salt and pepper to taste

Mix all the ingredients well and cook. Serve with crackers or toast. Add flour to thicken, if desired.

Tomato Delight

1 slice bacon
4 medium-sized onions

6 medium-sized potatoes
2 cups tomatoes
4 cups milk
salt and pepper to taste
a little flour

Cut the bacon in small pieces and fry. Chop the onions and brown it with the bacon. Add the potatoes and tomatoes cut into cubes. Add boiling water and cook till the potatoes are tender. Then add the milk and seasoning. Thicken with a little four and serve with toast, if desired.

~

French Fried Toast

1 egg
1 cup milk
a little salt
½ tsp baking powder
3 slices of bread

Combine all the ingredients (except the slices of bread) together. Dip the bread in the mixture and fry. Serve hot with syrup, if desired. It also tastes good served with sugar and cinnamon.

~

Cinnamon Toast

6 slices of toast
1 tsp cinnamon
2 tbsp sugar

Add enough cream to moisten the cinnamon and sugar. White the toast is still dry and hot, spread the mixed cream mixture over each toast.

◆

Savoury Toast

Mrs. L. B. Rambo

2 tbsp butter
2 tbsp flour
2 cups milk
1 cup cheese, finely chopped
salt and pepper

Toast 4 large slices or 8 halves of bread. Make a cream sauce by melting the butter, adding the flour and mixing well till it bubbles. Add the milk, gradually, stirring constantly. Cook till the mixture is smooth and thick. Add the cheese and stir till it melts. Add salt and pepper to taste and pour the sauce over the slices of toast. This will serve 4 people.

Do not let the cheese really cook or it will become tough and stringy. If desired, the slices of toast may be surrounded with tomato cut in slices and baked in the oven.

◆

Patty Shells

Mrs. Bauman

stale slices of bread
creamed meat or vegetables

Cut the slices of bread (stale) about 2'' thick. Shape into rounds by cutting off the corners with a knife, or a round cookie cutter. With a sharp knife, scoop out the centre till nearly the bottom. Drop the shells into hot fat and fry till golden brown on all sides. Or the shells may be toasted in the oven. Fill with creamed meat or vegetable. These can be made attractive for children by cutting the bread with animal-shaped cookie cutters.

—◆—

Cheese Aigrettes

Mrs. J. L. Gray

½ oz butter
1 gill water
1½ oz flour
1 oz cheese, grated
salt and cayenne
1 egg, separated
1 yolk

Heat the butter and water together. Bring the mixture to a boil. Remove from the fire. Add the sifted flour and mix till it forms a ball. Add the cheese and seasonings.

Beat in the eggs (separately). Heat the fat to barely smoking. Slide in batches small tsp of the mixture. Fry till golden brown. Repeat till all the batter is used up. Remove with a slotted spoon and drain. Arrange on a fancy paper and dust with cheese.

—◆—

Cheese Jalebis

Mrs. Clemes

4 eggs
1 cup flour
½ lb cheese, grated
½ cup milk
½ tsp salt

½ tsp lemon juice
¼ tsp dry mustard

Mix all the ingredients well and force a stream of batter through paper cones, form *jalebi* shapes and fry in deep fat. Serve warm or hot at tea, or for a cheese course at dinner.

Cheese Balls
Mrs. A. E. Anderson

2 oz butter
1 cup water
1 cup flour
½ cup cheese, grated
small quantity each salt, pepper and cayenne
3 eggs

Heat the butter with water in a saucepan and bring to a boil. Then add the flour and continue stirring till the mixture leaves the sides of the pan. Remove from the fire and allow the mixture to cool a little. Then stir in the cheese, pepper, salt and cayenne. Lastly, add the well-beaten eggs. Heat the fat in a deep pan and drop a tbsp of this mixture and fry till golden brown. Repeat till the mixture is over. Serve hot.

Lemon Cheese
Miss Grier

¼ lb butter
juice of 3 and grated rind of 2 lemons
¾ lb sugar
4 eggs

Put the butter in a jar standing in a dish of boiling water to melt. When the butter has melted, add the lemon juice, sugar, lemon rind and the beaten eggs. Cook till thick.

Vegetable and Fruit Club Sandwiches Miss Vance

For each plate, cut 3 slices of bread about 3/8" thick, toasted on one side and buttered on the other. Have 3 principal vegetables or fruits suitable for salads and other tasty things, such as celery, radish, pimento, olives, etc. A very good combination is beetroot, tomato and papaya. Place the lettuce leaves on the plate, a slice of the buttered and toasted bread, then cover it with sliced, cooked beetroot, with bits of celery and salad dressing. Place the second slice of toast covered with tomato and bits of radish and perhaps, a touch of onion and more salad dressing over the first. Add the third slice of toast covered with papaya and bits of pimento and olive and more salad dressing. Lastly, sprinkle some chopped walnuts. This makes a rather substantial meal by itself.

Grated Carrot Sandwiches

butter
4 tsp carrots, grated
1 tsp apple, grated

bread

Cream the butter and add the carrots and apple. Spread the mixture over the slices of bread.

Meat, Fowl and Fish

—◆—

A meatless man he has no meat,
Therefore he has no fat;
Yet I have meat, yet little I have,
I'm as lean as a basti cat.
But whether we're fat, or whether we're lean,
It's meat that we meet tonight;
And after we've met to have our meat,
Our meat'll be out of sight.

Beef Loaf

Mrs. A. E. Anderson

1 seer beef, finely ground
1 large onion, minced
2 eggs, well beaten
1 cup breadcrumbs
1 tbsp fat (lard or butter), melted
salt and pepper

Combine all the ingredients. Mix well kneading the mixture till smooth. Shape the mixture into a loaf. Bake for 1 hour in a moderate oven.

Corned Beef

2 seers beef
1 scant tsp saltpeter (sora)
4 tbsp salt
¼ lb molasses
1 large lemon

Work these ingredients into the meat turning it over and over for 2 or 3 days. Then boil until tender.

Beef en Casserole

Mrs. L. B. Rambo

1½ to 2 lb beef from the round
cut in pieces for stew
2 tsp salt
pepper
1 onion, sliced

1 carrot, diced
1 stalk of celery, finely cut
1 small can tomatoes, or fresh ones
1 turnip, diced
$1/_3$ cup flour
½ cup lard
2 tbsp flour (for the sauce)
2½ cups water

The vegetables may be varied to suit the taste. Put all the vegetables together in the bottom of a casserole. Season the meat and dredge with flour. Brown the meat in a frying pan, using a little lard. Then place the meat on top of the vegetables. Make a brown sauce in the frying pan by mixing a little butter, flour and water together. Cook till it thickens. Pour the sauce over the meat and vegetables. Cover the casserole and bake in a slow oven for 3 hours. Parboiled potatoes may be added ½ an hour before serving. Be sure that the sauce does not dry up.

Steamed Steak

Mrs. Riddle

1 lb steak
1 tsp sugar
2 tsp flour
1 tbsp vinegar
2 tbsp water
1 tsp Worcester sauce
a pinch of soda
salt and pepper to taste

Place the steak in a pie dish and add the remaining ingredients. Mix well. Cover the pie dish tightly and bake slowly for 3 hours or steam for 3 hours.

French Steak

1 lb tender beef steak, cut ½" thick
1 large onion, sliced
salt and pepper
3 large tomatoes, sliced
1 cup flour
2 tbsp fat

Pound the beef steak well. Sprinkle some salt, pepper and as much flour as you can pound in. Heat 2 tbsp *ghee* in a frying pan and brown the onion. Add the steak and fry till brown on both sides. Add the tomatoes, cover the mixture with water and simmer till the steak is tender. It makes its own gravy.

Spanish Steak

Mrs. E. Livengood

1 large slice round steak, 2" thick
6 large onions
6 large potatoes
2½ tbsp butter
1½ tsp salt
pepper to taste
1 cup milk

Grease a covered baking dish and place the steak in the bottom. Slice the onions and spread them over the steak. Slice the potatoes and spread them above the onions. Dot with butter. Add salt and pepper to taste, and cover the mixture with milk. Bake in a moderate oven for 2 hours.

Meat Soufflé (Serves: 6)   Mrs. Bauman

2 cups ground meat
2 tbsp butter
3 tbsp flour
¾ cup scalded milk or meat stock
½ tsp salt
3 egg yolks
3 egg whites

Melt the butter and add the flour. Mix well. Gradually, add the scalded milk or meat stock. Then add the salt and meat. Remove from the fire and add the egg yolks beaten till lemon coloured.

Cool the mixture and cut and fold in the egg whites beaten till stiff and dry. Pour the mixture in a buttered baking dish and bake for 20 minutes in a slow oven. Serve at once.

~·~

Ham in Apple Juice

2 slices of ham 1″ thick
1 cup syrup from apple pickles

Put the slices of ham in a dish. Pour the apple syrup over it. Bake for 45 minutes turning the slices of ham frequently.

~·~

Irish Stew (Serves: 5)   Mrs. Hansen

2 lb beef, cut in 1″ cubes
2 tbsp butter or shortening
2 tsp salt

pepper
enough water to cover the beef
5 large potatoes
plain crackers

Fry the beef in a buttered iron skillet for 3 minutes. Transfer the contents into a *degchi* (pot). Add salt and pepper and enough water to cover the beef. Boil for ¾ th of an hour. Then add the potatoes and as many plain crackers (that have a dab of butter in the centre) as you please. Cook till the potatoes are done. Serve hot.

~•~

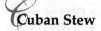 ## Cuban Stew

Mrs. Menzies

½ seer meat, diced
4 onions
¼ cup oil or *ghee*
4 tomatoes
2 tsp salt
pepper
(plus any other vegetable desired)

Fry the onions in the oil or *ghee* until brown. Add the tomatoes. Cook for a while then add the meat. Let it cook slowly for 1½ hours. Add just enough water to cover the mixture. When the meat is ¾th done, add the potatoes, carrots, beans or any other vegetables desired. Let the mixture simmer until almost done. Add salt and pepper and let it summer for 5 minutes more or until all is cooked.
Note: Green pepper, celery or parsley is a good addition. Makes a good meal.

~•~

Kofta Korma

Mrs. Y. Masik

1 *chattack bhune chane ki dal* (roasted Bengal gram)
1 seer minced mutton
2 tsp salt added to the minced meat
Masala: (all chopped fine and mixed together)
2 *chattack* coconut
4 *chattack* almonds
5 *choti elaichi* (green cardamom)
1 piece ginger
½ clove garlic
1 *chattack khuskhus* (poppy seeds)
1 or 2 pieces cinnamon sticks
1 or 2 green peppers
1 small red pepper

¼ seer *ghee* (clarified butter)
3 or 4 onions, finely sliced

Grind the roasted Bengal gram and add the minced mutton. Mix thoroughly. Then mix in half of the mixed masala. Divide the mixture into 2 equal balls.

Melt the *ghee* on a mild fire in a pan. Add the onions and let them brown. Put in the remaining half of the masala and cook until a reddish colour is obtained. Add the meat balls. Cook covered, until the balls are done, then stir carefully and add enough water to make a thick gravy. Let the mixture cook for about 15 minutes. Serve with hot steamed rice.

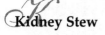

Kidney Stew

Mrs. J. L. Gray

1 kidney, cut into small cubes
1 large onion, chopped
6 medium-sized potatoes, cut into cubes

¾ tsp salt
pepper
2 tbsp flour

In a bowl, mix the kidney and onion. Cover with water and boil the mixture till partly done. Then add the potatoes, salt and pepper to taste. When the potatoes are done, stir in the flour mixed with cold water. Add enough water to make a thick gravy. Serve with toast.

❦

Potted Meat

2 lb good steak
½ lb ham
½ lb butter
3 tbsp anchovy sauce
2 tsp white pepper
3 tsp salt
1 tsp mace, ground
½ nutmeg, ground

Cut the beef and ham into small pieces. Put them in a pan with the other ingredients. Cover and steam for 4 hours. Strain the gravy and put the rest through a mincer 3 times. Now add the gravy and mix well. Transfer into small pots and cover with paper.

❦

Baked Hash

Mrs. D. T. Miller

1 cup cold meat, beef or ham, chopped
2 cups rice, boiled
1 cup tomatoes, stewed
½ cup breadcrumbs
2 eggs, beaten
2 tbsp butter, melted

Mix all the ingredients together except the butter. Then pour the melted butter in a baking dish. Add the mixture and bake in a moderate oven.

Scalloped Meat

M. N. Harne

4 cups rice, boiled
2 cups leftover meat
1 tsp salt
¼ tsp pepper
1 tbsp parsley
¼ tsp onion juice
1 egg
¼ cup bread or cracker crumbs

Combine all the ingredients in a bowl (except rice) and mix well. Spread alternate layers of rice and the mixture. Steam for about 1 hour.

Hungarian Goulash

3 lb beef, cut into 1" cubes
1 tbsp lard
1 tsp salt
1 tsp paprika
1 tsp caraway seeds
1 cup onions
1 cup carrots
1 cup celery
4 cups potatoes
a few parsley leaves, finely chopped

Heat the lard in a pan. Add the beef, salt, paprika, caraway seeds and onions. Let the mixture cook slowly for 1 hour. Add the carrots, celery, potatoes and enough water to cover the mixture. Cook till done. Serve garnished with parsley leaves.

Cottage Meat Pie

seasoned mashed potatoes
creamed meat (or bits of meat
moistened with milk)

Line the bottom of a baking dish with mashed potatoes. Add a thick layer of creamed meat. Cover with another layer of mashed potatoes. Bake till the mixture is heated through.

Curry Puffs

½ seer lean meat, ground
1 small onion
2 tbsp *ghee*
$1/_3$ clove garlic (if desired)
1 tbsp curry powder
2 lb grate coconut
For the pastry
1 cup flour
1 tsp lard or butter
¼ tsp salt
a little cold water

Fry the onion in *ghee*, add the garlic, if desired, curry powder, coconut and the meat. Cook covered until the meat is tender, stirring once in a while. Do not use water.

Make a dough with the flour, butter, salt and a little water. Divide the dough into lemon-sized balls. Roll each out into thin discs and put 1 tbsp of the mixture into each and seal. Deep-fry these puffs in fat till golden.

❦

Chicken Pudding
Jennie E. Crozier

1 young stewed chicken
2 tbsp parsley, minced
2 hard-boiled eggs, sliced
1 tsp onion juice with chicken broth to moisten

Put the chicken, cut in pieces, in a buttered baking dish. Add the parsley, hard-boiled eggs and onion juice with chicken broth. Mix well. Prepare the following mixture:

2 cups flour
1 tsp baking powder
a pinch of salt
2 eggs, beaten light
1 cup milk
1 tbsp butter, melted

Sift the flour, baking powder and salt together. Add the eggs, milk and butter. Mix well, pour over the chicken and bake.

—◆—

Roast Chicken (Serves: 2-4)

1½ or 2 lb broiler chicken
salad oil
salt and pepper

Cut the broiler in half and brush salad oil all over. Sprinkle salt and pepper, then arrange the halves skin side up in a small baking pan. Bake in a moderately hot oven for 25 minutes. Then turn the flesh side up, fill the cavity of each with stuffing and brush some salad oil all over again. Return to the oven and bake for 30 minutes more or until tender.

—◆—

Stuffing for Fowl   A. B. Cowdry

1 cup butter, melted
1 medium-sized bunch of celery, finely cut
2 onions, finely cut
giblets, finely cut
1 loaf of stale bread

salt and pepper
sage
raisins, if desired

Heat the butter; add celery, onions and giblets. Simmer until done, but not brown. Crumble the slices of bread, finely. Moisten the crumbs with water and squeeze dry. Pour the butter mixture over the breadcrumbs, mix well, season to taste with salt, pepper and sage. Add raisins, if desired.

Note: An apple in the neck of a fowl adds flavour to it.

❧

Jellied Chicken   Gladys Holmes

1 good-sized chicken, cooked
salt and pepper
parsley
½ oz gelatin soaked in 2 tbsp water for ½ hour
2 carrots, sliced
1 turnip, sliced
lettuce, sliced
1 tbsp Bovril
2 hard-boiled eggs

Chop the meat of the chicken finely, omitting the back and inferior parts. Season to taste and sprinkle chopped parsley. Put the gelatin in a pan with the carrots, turnip, lettuce, Bovril, adding 1 pt cold water. Boil everything together for ½ an hour and strain. Add this mixture to the chicken. Rinse out a mould with cold water, line it with slices of hard-boiled eggs and pour the mixture over it. Serve on lettuce leaves placed on a dish.

❧

Scalloped Salmon

Indiana Cookbook

1 can salmon
1 pt milk
2 tbsp butter
2 tbsp flour
salt and pepper to taste
breadcrumbs

Boil the milk in a pan. Melt the butter in another pan and stir in the flour. When the milk starts to boil, add the butter and flour mixture. Add salt and pepper to taste. Cook till the mixture resembles a custard. Then line this mixture in a buttered baking dish, covered with a layer of salmon, then another layer of the milk mixture and so on till the dish is full. The last layer should be of the milk mixture. Sprinkle some breadcrumbs dusted with salt and pepper and bits of butter. Bake in a moderate oven for 1½ hours or until brown.

Salmon Mould

Mrs. Strickler

1 can salmon
1 tbsp butter, melted
4 eggs, lightly beaten
½ cup breadcrumbs
salt, pepper and minced parsley

Chop the salmon finely. Add the butter and breadcrumbs mixed with beaten eggs. Add salt, pepper and parsley. Mix well. Transfer the mixture into a buttered mould and steam for about 1 hour.

Vegetables

—◆—

THE POTATO

A sailor went sailing over the Tay
By the name of Edgar Poe;
And he stubbed his poor digit on a root
Which is now the Poe-tay-toe.

Dr. G. E. Miller

Sweet Potatoes with Almonds

6 sweet potatoes
3 tbsp butter
½ tsp salt
½ cup cream
¼ cup almonds, chopped

Boil and mash the potatoes. Add the butter and season with salt. Add the cream and beat until light. Mix in the almonds and bake.

—◦—

Potato Chips

Peel and finely slice the potatoes. Wash and pat them dry with a cloth. Drop them gently into a pan with smoking hot oil, and fry till light golden. Remove with a slotted spoon and drain the excess oil on absorbent kitchen towels. Sprinkle some salt and serve.

—◦—

French Fried Potatoes

Peel and cut the potatoes lengthwise, about ½'' thick. Wash and pat them dry with a cloth. Drop them gently into a pan with hot oil, and fry till golden. Remove with a slotted spoon and drain in a colander or on absorbent kitchen towels.

—◦—

Scalloped Potatoes

10 medium-sized potatoes
salt and pepper
flour
butter
sweet milk

Peel and finely slice the potatoes. Arrange them in layers in a baking dish, adding between the layers salt, pepper, flour and bits of butter. When the dish is nearly full, cover with sweet milk and bake in an oven until the potatoes are soft.

—◆—

Stuffed Baked Potatoes

1.   6 or 8 large potatoes, baked
$^1/_3$ cup milk
1 onion finely chopped
parsley, finely chopped
salt and pepper

Carefully cut off one end of the potato and scoop out the inside. Mash the scooped portion, adding milk, onion, parsley, salt and pepper. Mix thoroughly and then carefully refill the potato shells with this mixture. Keep hot in the oven.

2.   6 or 8 large potatoes, baked
1 tbsp butter
¼ cup hot milk
1 tsp salt
pepper
2 egg whites, beaten

Chop one end of the potato and carefully scoop out the inside. Mash the scooped part, adding butter, hot milk, salt and pepper. Mix thoroughly. Add the beaten egg whites. Stir gently and carefully refill the potato shells with this mixture. Brown the stuffed potatoes in the oven.

3. Mash the potatoes as above and add ¼ cup grated cheese. Refill the potato shells and keep hot in the oven till served.

Potato Puff

Mrs. Whitlock

2 lb potatoes, boiled
2 eggs, separated
½ small onion, finely chopped
3 oz cheese, grated
salt and pepper
2 tbsp milk
2 oz butter

Mash the potatoes and add the beaten egg yolks. Add the onion, cheese, salt, pepper, milk and butter. Mix well and then fold in the stiffly-beaten egg whites. Carefully transfer the mixture into a well-greased fire-proof dish and bake in a hot oven for 20 minutes. This must be served immediately.

Potato Cakes

1 cup thickly cooked dal well seasoned
½ cup cheese, grated
½ cup breadcrumbs
mashed potatoes
vegetable oil

To the cooked dal, mix in the cheese and some bread-crumbs to hold the mixture together. Divide the mixture equally into small cakes. Cover each cake with a layer of mashed potatoes. Roll them in breadcrumbs and then fry in a little oil until golden brown. This can be served with spinach for lunch.

❧—

Pimento Potatoes

mashed potatoes
3 mashed pimentos
¼ pt cream
¼ pt milk
1 tbsp butter
salt and pepper

Mix all the ingredients thoroughly and beat well.

❧—

Indian Potato Curry   Mrs. Donald

2 seers potatoes, peeled, cut into pieces
2 pice weight green coriander
1 pice weight garam masala
1 piece coconut 2½" by 1"
a little turmeric powder
1 piece green ginger about 2" long
1 pod of garlic
a little red pepper
1 onion, chopped
some *ghee* (clarified butter)

Grind together all the ingredients except the potatoes, onion and *ghee*. Heat some *ghee* in a pan. Add the onion and fry till brown, then add the ground ingredients. Fry for 5 to 10 minutes. Now add the potatoes and fry for a while, but do not brown. Add salt and just about enough water to cook the potatoes and to have a thick gravy.

Chilli Con Carne

E. L. Moody

1 pt red dry beans
1 lb lean beef
2 oz suet
1 sweet red pepper
1 small onion
salt
$1/8$ tsp mustard
a little vinegar

Soak the beans overnight. In the morning, arrange them in a pot with the solid meat or cut into small pieces, suet, red pepper, cut in rings, and the onion in pieces. Add the salt to taste. Add the mustard mixed with vinegar and a dash of cayenne, if desired. Cover with water and bake slowly for 3 or 4 hours in a moderate oven.

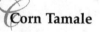

Corn Tamale

M. McGee

1 can corn
1 cup yellow corn meal
5 ripe or ½ can tomatoes
1½ cups sweet milk

1 green pepper
1 onion, chopped
2 eggs, well beaten
1 dozen ripe olives
½ tsp red pepper
1 tsp black pepper

Mix all the ingredients together. Add a little cold meat or chicken, if desired. Transfer the mixture to a loaf tin and bake for 45 minutes.

❧

Scalloped Corn

Mrs. Strickler

1 can corn
2 eggs
1 tbsp flour
1 tbsp butter
1 tbsp sugar
1 cup milk
salt

Mix all the ingredients together and bake for 30 minutes.

❧

Corn Fritters

R. C. Newton

1 can corn
½ tsp salt
1 cup flour
¾ cup milk
1 heaped tsp baking powder

Mix all the ingredients together. Fry the same way as you do pancakes.

—◆—

Stuffed Peppers

5 green peppers, halved
4 large tomatoes, cut in pieces
3 onions, chopped
1 cup olives, chopped
1 can corn
2 cups crackers or breadcrumbs
2 lb potatoes, boiled, shredded
salt, pepper and butter

Mix all the ingredients well and stuff into the green pepper shells. Bake till brown.

—◆—

Eggplant Stew

1 large eggplant
1 onion
3 stalks celery
1/3 cup rice
1 tomato
1 qt boiling water
1 tsp butter
salt and pepper

Cut the eggplant in pieces and soak in slightly salt water for 15 minutes. Then boil for 15 minutes. Add the onion, celery, rice and tomato. Mix well. Pour in the boiling water and cook for 1½ hours. Add the butter and check for seasoning.

Baked Eggplant

boiled eggplant
1 tbsp cracker crumbs
1 tsp butter
salt and pepper
1 egg

Boil the eggplant until soft and mash finely. To each cup of mashed eggplant, add 1 tbsp cracker crumbs and 1 tsp butter, salt and pepper. Transfer the mixture into a baking dish. Beat the egg and spread it over the mashed eggplant mixture. Sprinkle with crumbs and bake till brown.

Eggplant

1. Slice in thin pieces. Dip them in batter made of flour, water, pepper and salt, and fry. Serve at once.

2. Peel and cut into pieces. Boil till tender Then mash and add 1 or 2 eggs, cracker or breadcrumbs, salt and pepper. Dip a spoonful of this mixture in hot oil and fry.

3. Fry the onion in *ghee*. Add the chopped eggplant and tomato and cook till done. Add salt and pepper.

4. Cut up the eggplant in cubes (3 cups) and fry in butter. Put in a baking dish covered with boiled noodles or macaroni. Bake in an oven.

Tomato and Okra Stew

1 pt okra, sliced
1 large onion
2 tbsp fat
1 pt tomatoes
green pepper, if desired
salt to taste

Boil the okra for a few minutes in water with a tsp of vinegar, then drain. Brown the sliced onion in the fat, add the okra and brown slightly. Add the tomatoes and green pepper and cook till done. Season to taste. Cook slowly for better results.

Stuffed Tomatoes

2 cups breadcrumbs
2 cups potatoes, boiled, mashed
3 tbsp melted butter
1 yolk of hard-boiled egg
1 onion, finely minced
2 tsp mixed prepared mustard with tomato pulp
pepper and salt
scooped out tomato shells

Mix the breadcrumbs, mashed potatoes, butter, egg, onion, mustard and tomato pulp. Sprinkle salt, pepper and sugar into each shell. Then stuff the tomato shells with this breadcrumb mixture. Transfer the tomato shells into a greased baking dish and sprinkle some breadcrumbs. Bake for ½ an hour.

Boston Baked Beans

3 cups beans
1 medium-sized onion
½ cup molasses
1 tsp mustard
salt
2 tbsp butter or *ghee*

Soak the beans for several hours and then boil for about 10 to 15 minutes. In a baking dish, arrange a layer of beans, onion, molasses, mustard, salt and butter or *ghee*. Bake covered in the oven for 8 to 10 hours. More or less molasses can be added according to taste.

Spinach and Cheese

1 lb spinach
2 tsp lemon juice
1 oz butter
pepper and salt
2 oz fine white breadcrumbs
3 oz cheese, finely grated

Wash the spinach and cook in a pan with 1 tsp lemon juice. Let it cook in its own water for 15 minutes. Drain well and when cool chop finely, and return it to the pan. Stir in the butter, the remaining lemon juice and season with pepper and salt. Grease a baking dish, sprinkle a layer of mixed breadcrumbs and grated cheese then a layer of spinach, and continue with alternate layers till the dish is full. The final layer should be of breadcrumbs and cheese. Dust with pepper and salt. Dot with butter and bake for 25 minutes.

Macaroni and Tomatoes

1 cup macaroni, boiled
2 tbsp butter
2 tbsp flour
½ tsp pepper
salt to taste
2 cups tomatoes, stewed
¼ tsp onion, chopped

Heat the butter in a pan; add the flour and seasoning and gradually, the stewed tomatoes and onion. Cook until the mixture is smooth. Remove from the flame and pour this mixture over the boiled macaroni or place in a baking dish and bake in a moderate oven for 15 to 20 minutes.

—✦—

Baked Beans with Tomato Sauce

1 qt beans
1 can tomatoes
15 whole cloves
1 onion, thinly sliced
salt and pepper
1 tbsp molasses
1 piece of bacon, optional

Boil the beans for ½ an hour. Cook the tomatoes, cloves and onion in a skillet until the onion is soft. Press this tomato and onion mixture through a sieve and pour over the boiled beans. Add a little salt and pepper, molasses and bacon. Then cover and bake for 5 or 6 hours. Add water if the mixture becomes too dry. When done, the beans should be of a pink colour and covered with a dressing that looks like tomato ketchup.

Tamale Beans

1 pt beans
1 pt tomatoes
1 small onion
2 cloves garlic
1 tbsp olive oil
1 or 2 lb pork or beef, cut in cubes

Soak the beans overnight. Parboil. Add the other ingredients and simmer for 2 hours longer. Add 1 or 2 tsp pepper, salt and water. Bake for 1 hour.

Dumplings

2 cups flour
2 tsp creamed butter
1 tsp soda
½ tsp salt
2 tbsp butter (work in)
¾ cup milk

Mix all the ingredients together and knead into a soft dough. Cut the dough into ½" thick pieces and drop the dumplings into any boiling stock. Boil for 10 minutes.

Fried Okra

Cut into thin slices crosswise and fry in fat. Drain thoroughly and sprinkle with salt and pepper.

Okra and Tomato

Cut up the okra and tomato and boil them together till tender. Add salt, pepper and butter.

Cabbage Rice and Poached Eggs   Mrs. J. L. Gray

6 or 8 oz tender cabbage
1 oz fat
1 small onion, shredded
1 gill water
salt
½ gill rice
1 or 2 eggs

Heat the fat and add the onion. Stir fry. Add the cabbage, half of the water and salt. Cook slowly. When the cabbage is half cooked, add the rice and mix well, then add the remaining water. Continue cooking until the rice is tender. A few minutes before serving, poach the eggs and serve on top of the cabbage rice.

Baked Lentil   E. L. Moody

lentil
4 slices of bacon
salt and pepper

Partly cook the lentil and transfer it into a baking dish and top with slices of bacon, salt and pepper to taste. Bake in an oven.

Note: A few sliced okra can be added, if desired.

Vegetable Hash (Serves: 6)   Mrs. H. E. Wylie

3 tbsp fat
½ cup onion, chopped
3 cups cabbage, chopped
1 cup rice, cooked
2 cups tomatoes, stewed
salt and pepper

Heat 3 tbsp fat in a frying pan; add the onion and cook till tender, but not brown. Add the cabbage and cook for 15 minutes. Add water, if necessary. Add the rice and tomatoes. Cook slowly till the cabbage is tender. Season to taste.

<hr>

Baked Cream Winter Squash

squash
salt and pepper
butter
flour
sweet milk

Peel and slice the squash. Arrange a layer of squash in a baking dish with salt and pepper, butter and flour. Repeat till the dish is full. Pour enough sweet milk to cover the mixture. Bake in a slow oven.

<hr>

Spinach Ring (Serves: 8-12)

3 cups spinach, cooked, well drained
4 eggs, beaten
¼ cup milk

¼ cup margarine, melted
1 tsp sugar
½ tsp salt

To the beaten eggs, add the milk, margarine, sugar and salt. Chop the cooked spinach finely and add to the egg mixture. Pack this mixture into a greased ring mould. Set the mould in a pan of water and bake at 350°F for 1 hour or till set. To serve, invert the mould on a platter, fill the centre with creamed cauliflower and garnish with pieces of tomato.

❧━━━◆━━━☙

Spinach Cakes (Serves: 4)   Vesta Miller

1¼ cups spinach, cooked, drained, chopped
1 hard-boiled egg
1 tsp salt
a pinch of pepper
1 egg, well beaten
breadcrumbs
1 cup thin white sauce
1 onion, chopped

Mix the spinach with the chopped hard-boiled egg white. Add salt, pepper and egg. Let the mixture stand for 15 minutes to stiffen. When stiff, divide it equally into lemon-sized balls and shape each into patties. Roll the patties over the breadcrumbs and fry them in hot fat until brown.

For the white sauce, heat 1 tbsp butter, add 1 tbsp flour and cook until smooth but not brown. Gradually, add 1 cup milk, stirring all the time. Cook until slightly thick. Remove from the flame and add the onion. Pour the sauce over the patties and garnish with hard-boiled egg yolk.

━━━◆━━━

Salads and Salad Dressings

Two boiled potatoes strained through a kitchen sieve,
Softness and smoothness to a salad give
Of mordant mustard take a single spoon
Distrust the condiment that bites too soon
Yet deem it not, thou man of taste a fault,
To add a double quantity of salt.
Four times the spoon with oil of lucca crown,
And twice with vinegar procured from town;
True taste requires it, and your poet begs
The pounded yellow of two well-boiled eggs.
Let onions atoms lurk within the bowl,
And, scarce suspected, animate the whole.
And lastly in the flavoured compound toss.
A magic spoonful of anchovy sauce.
Oh great and glorious, Oh herbaceous meat,
Would tempt the dying anchorite to eat
Back to the world he'd turn his weary soul,
And plunge his fingers in the salad bowl.'

Sydney Smith

Club House Salad

E. L. Moody

1 packet macaroni
1 dozen sweet small pickles
1 tin pimentos
salt

Boil the macaroni in hot water. Drain. Cut the pickles and pimentos in small pieces. Add any salad dressing (and a little cream, if desired) and salt to taste. Mix well and serve on lettuce leaves.

Marshmallow Salad

1 cup marshmallow, diced
1 head lettuce
$^1/_3$ cup pineapple, diced
$^1/_3$ cup apricots, diced
¼ tsp salt
2 tbsp lemon juice
$^1/_3$ cup peaches, diced
¼ cup whipped cream
½ tsp paprika on top just before serving

Roll the marshmallows in powdered sugar. Combine all the ingredients in a bowl and mix well.

Salmon Salad

E. L. Moody

1 can salmon
4 hard-boiled eggs

1 egg yolk, raw
2 tsp oil or melted butter
salt and red pepper

Mash the hard-boiled egg yolks and mix in the raw egg yolk.
Add a little vinegar to make a paste. Add the oil and salmon
and mix well. Serve this on lettuce leaves. Chop the hard-
boiled egg whites and either mix it in or sprinkle over the top
of the salad. Check for seasoning. Peanuts may be added, if
desired.

Carrot Salad

2 cups carrots, finely chopped
1 cup celery, chopped
2 hard-boiled eggs, cut into pieces
½ cup peanuts

Combine all the ingredients and mix with mayonnaise
dressing. Serve on lettuce leaves.

Fruit Salad

5 oranges, peeled, segments separated
5 bananas, peeled, chopped
1 can pineapple
½ packet clear gelatin soaked in 1 pt water
1 pt sugar
2 lemon juice

In a pan, boil the water mixed with gelatin, sugar and lemon
juice. When the sugar dissolves, remove the mixture from the

flame. Strain, and pour this liquid over the fruits and let the mixture stand to set.

❦

Cheese Salad

Mrs. Shaw

1 tbsp gelatin
½ cup cold water
½ cup pineapple, grated
½ cup cheese, grated
½ cup cream
½ cup olives
salt and pepper

Soak the gelatin in water. Cook the pineapple and add the gelatin mixture. Then add cheese, cream, olives and check for seasoning. Mix well and serve.

❦

Pineapple Marshmallow Salad

E. L. Moody

Cut the pineapple in small pieces and add the marshmallows, cut in cubes. Mix with any salad dressing and serve.

❦

Banana Salad

Peel the bananas and cut in halves, lengthwise. Place on lettuce leaves. Sprinkle with ground or salted peanuts. Cover with mayonnaise dressing and sprinkle some more peanuts on top.

Green Pepper and Cheese Salad   Miss Vance

1 cup cooked *suji* (semolina)
1.2 lb fresh cream cheese
salt and pepper

Mix all the ingredients together and heat till the mixture is
well blended. With a sharp knife, scoop out the insides of the
sweet green peppers. Fill the cheese mixture into the green
pepper shells. Cut in ½ " thick slices.

Place them on lettuce leaves and add a salad dressing of
your choice.

Note: The above mixture can be cut in cubes and added to
the other salads as well.

Salad Dressing   M. McGee

4 tbsp butter, melted
1 tbsp flour
1 cup sweet milk
1 tbsp salt
2 tbsp sugar
1 tsp mustard
1 egg
½ cup vinegar

Heat the butter and mix in the flour. Stir till smooth, then add
the milk and let it boil. Add the other ingredients together.
Vinegar should be added last. Mix well.

Uncooked Salad Dressing

Miss Forbes

2 eggs
1 tsp salt
1 tsp dry mustard
1 can condensed milk
1 cup vinegar

Beat the eggs, add salt and mustard. Add the condensed milk and vinegar and beat well. Store in a jar.

Boiled Mayonnaise Dressing

Mrs. E. C. Lochlin

4 egg yolks or 2 whole eggs
½ tsp dry mustard
1 tbsp flour
3 tbsp sugar
1 tsp salt
1 tbsp butter
½ cup vinegar
½ cup water

Mix all the dry ingredients together. Add the butter, vinegar and water. Boil the mixture over a pan of hot water till smooth. Put a few spoonfuls into the beaten yolks. Mix thoroughly then stir in the remainder of the sauce. Cook on low heat till the sauce thickens, stirring constantly. When ready, add a little cream or lemon juice. If desired, beat in as much oil as it will hold from ½ to 1 cup.

Butter or Sour Milk Salad Dressing   Mrs. Donald

1½ cups sour milk
1 heaped tbsp flour
1 tsp mustard
1 tsp salt and pepper
1 heaped tbsp sugar
butter, size of a walnut
1 egg, well beaten

Boil all the ingredients together, stirring constantly till it gets fairly thick. Then add ½ cup vinegar and boil till thick.

—❦—

Cooked Mayonnaise Dressing   Mrs. A. E. Anderson

2 egg yolks
½ tsp dry mustard
1 tsp salt
1 cup salad oil
1 tsp sugar (more if desired)
3 tbsp vinegar

Place all the ingredients in a bowl, but do not mix. Add either vinegar or lemon juice.

Meanwhile, cook 2 tbsp butter with 3 tbsp flour and when smooth, add 1 cup hot water and boil in a double boiler for 10 minutes. Add this to the above mixture and beat with an egg beater till smooth and velvety.

Chilli sauce, grated onion, chopped olives or pickle may be added for seasoning depending on your salad.

—❦—

Nestle's Milk Salad Dressing   O. B. Dodds

2 eggs, well beaten
1 tin Nestle's milk
¾ cup vinegar
¼ tsp mustard
1 tsp salt

Beat all the ingredients together with an egg beater for 2 or 3 minutes. No cooking is required.

Creamless Salad Dressing   M. R. Long

2 eggs, well beaten
½ cup vinegar
3½ tbsp sugar
¾ cup water
1 tsp salt
1 tbsp butter
1 tsp flour
1½ tsp mustard

Combine all the ingredients together and cook in a double boiler till the mixture thickens.

Salad Dressing   Miss Vance

2 eggs, well beaten
1 can sweet condensed milk
½ cup butter, melted but not hot
½ tsp salt

½ tsp prepared mustard
½ cup vinegar

Combine all the ingredients in the above order. Mix well.

Boiled Salad Dressing

Mrs. Harrington

3 tbsp flour
3 tbsp sugar
½ tbsp salt
¼ tsp mustard
4 eggs yolk or 2 whole eggs
4 cups milk
½ cup vinegar

Mix all the dry ingredients together. Add the beaten eggs and milk. Cook in a double boiler till the mixture coats the spoon. Add the vinegar. Cook for a minute and then remove from the flame.

Salad Dressing (Serves: 40)

1 cup sugar
6 tsp salt
4 tsp mustard
1 tsp white pepper

Mix all the dry ingredients together. Add 3 eggs, beaten till thick, 4 cups sour thick cream and 2 cups vinegar. Cook the mixture over a pan of hot water until creamy. This dressing will keep for a year.

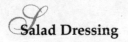# Salad Dressing

R. C. Newton

1 cup sugar
1 tbsp flour
1 tbsp salt
1 tbsp mustard
½ cup vinegar
3 eggs

Mix the dry ingredients, then add the vinegar. Mix well and add this mixture to the well-beaten eggs and cook in a double boiler, stirring constantly. This is a stock dressing and should be diluted well with whipped cream.

Low-calorie Salad Dressing

4 tbsp lemon juice
3 tbsp water
½ tsp salt
a pinch of pepper
½ tsp sugar
1 garlic clove, optional
½ tsp mustard, optional
2 tbsp salad oil, optional

Mix all the ingredients and store in a jar for a minimum of 30 minutes to blend the flavours. Serve 1 tsp of this dressing per person.

Puddings and Desserts

—❦—

THE NUT

I am the nut. When cracked, at my best,
I tickle the spot right under the vest.
Without, I confess I am rather austere;
But my heart is all right, and brim-full of cheer.
When filled to the neck, and weary of food,
Folk give me a taste, and consider me good.

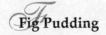 Fig Pudding

Mrs. J. L. Gray

½ lb figs, washed, chopped
¼ lb sugar
¼ lb suet, shredded
¼ lb flour
½ tsp soda
a pinch of salt
2 eggs
½ tsp cream of tartar
milk

Mix the figs with the sugar. Add the suet and all the dry ingredients. Beat the eggs with the cream of tartar. Add a little milk to obtain a soft consistency and then pour this to the above mixture. Turn this into a greased mould and steam for 2 hours. When done, invert the mould over a hot dish and serve with fig sauce (see recipe below).

½ pt water
6 oz sugar
4 figs, chopped

Boil the water and sugar together till the sugar dissolves. Add the figs and simmer for about 1 minute. Serve with the fig pudding.

Suet Pudding

M. M. Saum

1 cup suet
1 cup molasses
1 cup sour milk
2¾ cups flour
1½ tsp soda

1½ tsp salt
1 tsp cinnamon
½ tsp cloves
¾ cup currants

Add the molasses and sour milk to the suet. Add 2 cups of flour sifted with soda, salt and the spices. Add the currants mixed with the remaining flour. Turn the mixture into a buttered mould. Cover and steam for 4 hours.

———

Rock Cream or Spanish Cream   M. Manry

2 tbsp gelatin
1 qt milk
3 eggs, separated
1 cup sugar
vanilla

Soak the gelatin in milk and cook till it comes to a boil. Then stir in the beaten egg yolks and sugar. Cook for a few minutes. Remove from the fire, fold in the beaten egg whites. Add the vanilla and transfer the mixture to a mould.

———

Light Pudding   Mrs. Donald

2 tbsp butter
1 egg
2½ tbsp sugar
¾ cup milk
vanilla
3 tbsp baking powder
1½ cups flour

Mix all the ingredients together and steam for 1 hour. Serve with chocolate sauce (see recipe below).

> 2 cups water
> 1 tbsp flour
> ½ cups sugar
> 1 tbsp butter
> a little vanilla
> 1¼ tbsp cocoa

Mix all the ingredients together and bring it to a boil. Remove from the flame and pour over the pudding and serve.

Tapioca Pudding

> 3 tbsp tapioca
> 1 qt milk
> 4 eggs, separated
> 1 cup sugar
> 4 tbsp coconut

Soak the tapioca overnight in a little water. Add the milk and boil for ½ an hour. Add the beaten egg yolks mixed with sugar and 3 tbsp coconut. Boil for 10 minutes longer, then pour into a baking dish. Fold in the beaten egg whites and top with 2 tbsp of sugar and 1 tbsp of coconut. Bake till brown.

Pineapple Caramel Pudding

A. B. Cowdry

3 eggs
1 cup granulated sugar
½ cup canned pineapple juice
1 tsp vanilla
1 cup flour
1 tsp baking powder
$^{1}/_{3}$ tsp salt
4 pineapple, slices
½ cup brown sugar

Beat the eggs until with the sugar till very light. Add the pineapple juice, vanilla and the dry ingredients sifted together. Arrange the slices of pineapple in a flat pan or mould which has been generously greased with butter. Sprinkle the brown sugar over the fruit and pour in the egg mixture. Bake in a moderate oven at 350-375°F for 30-35 minutes. To serve, invert on to a plate at once. The pudding may be eaten hot or cold.

Steamed Carrot Pudding

E. L. Moody

1 cup potato, grated
1 cup seeded raisins
2 cups carrots, grated
1 tsp salt
1 cup suet, chopped
1 tsp soda
1 cup brown sugar
½ tsp baking powder
½ tsp each cinnamon, cloves, nutmeg
juice of 1 lemon

Combine all the ingredients and mix well. Steam for 3 hours. Serve with a clear sauce.

~

Float

1 qt fresh milk
4 eggs, separated
1 cup sugar
1 tbsp cornflour

Bring the milk to a boil. Then add the beaten yolks mixed with sugar, cornflour and a little cold milk. When the mixture begins to thicken, remove from the fire. Stir in the vanilla and the beaten egg whites.

~

Hurst's Pudding

3 eggs
¼ cup sugar
3 tbsp cream
½ cup flour
½ tsp soda
1 cup preserves
½ tsp nutmeg

Beat the eggs and add sugar, cream, flour and soda mixed in a little water. Add the preserves and bake in a baking dish.

~

Baked Fruit Pudding

Pile sweetened fruit in a 1" or more deep baking dish. Cream together 1 cup sugar with 2 tbsp butter. Add 1 egg, 1 cup milk, 2 cups flour, 2 tsp cream of tartar and 1 tsp soda. Flavour with nutmeg or lemon. Pour over the fruit and bake. Turn the cake upside down on a plate and serve with lemon sauce.

Snow Pudding
E. L. Moody

2 tbsp sugar mixed with 3 tbsp cornflour
1 pt boiling water
1 egg, separated
½ tsp vanilla
1 cup sweet milk
1 tbsp flour

Pour the boiling water over the sugar and cornflour mixture, and cook for 5 minutes, stirring constantly. Add the beaten egg whites and vanilla. Pour the mixture in a wet dish. Set aside to cool. Make a custard by cooking the egg yolks with 2 tbsp sugar, 1 cup sweet milk and 1 tbsp flour. Let the mixture come to a boil. Remove from the fire. When ready to serve, pour the custard over the pudding. Serve cold.

English Steamed Pudding
Mrs. E. Livengood

1 cup carrots, grated
1½ cups flour
1 cup potatoes, grated

1 tsp soda, dissolved in a little warm water
1 cup raisins
1 cup sugar
¾ cups preserved lemon rind or
1 cup currants
1 cup suet, chopped
salt to taste

Mix all the ingredients thoroughly and steam for 3 hours.

＊

Boiled Custard

3 egg yolks
¼ cup sugar
$1/_3$ tsp salt
2 cups scalded milk
½ tsp vanilla

Beat the egg yolks slightly. Add the sugar and salt. Pour the scalded milk over the egg yolk mixture, stirring constantly. Cook the mixture over a pan of hot water, stirring constantly till it thickens and a coating forms on the spoon. Strain and cool. Add the vanilla.

Note: ½ tbsp cornstarch may be used instead of 1 egg yolk, if eggs are scarce.

＊

Date and Nut Torte   Mrs. A. E. Parker

2 eggs
1 cup sugar
1 tsp vanilla

1 cup dates, ground
1 cup walnuts
$^1/_3$ cup flour
1 tbsp baking powder
¼ tsp salt

Beat together the eggs, sugar and vanilla. In another bowl, mix the dates, walnuts, flour, baking powder and salt. To this add the egg mixture and bake for about ½ an hour.

Serve with cream.

Date Surprise

M. McGee

½ cup sugar
2 cups milk
1 tbsp butter

Mix all the ingredients in a double boiler and bring to a boil. Add 2 tbsp cornstarch or 1 egg. Moisten with cold milk. Cook till the mixture thickens, but is not too stiff. Add 1 cup dates, a few drops of almond extract and 1 tsp vanilla. Pour the mixture into glasses and when cold serve with whipped cream and a piece of date on top.

Black Pudding

Mrs. E. Livengood

½ cup cold water
1 egg
1 cup molasses
1 tbsp butter
1¼ cups flour

1 tsp soda
1 cup raisins
a pinch of salt
a pinch of cinnamon

Mix all the ingredients together and steam for 1 hour.

— ❧ —

Cottage Pudding

Indiana Cookbook

1 cup sugar
2 cups flour
1 cup milk
1 egg
butter, size of a walnut
2 tsp baking powder

Mix all the ingredients together. Bake in a hot oven.

— ❧ —

English Plum Pudding

1 lb seeded raisins
6 eggs
1 lb currants
2 tbsp salt
½ lb citron, chopped
1 lb brown sugar
1 lb suet
1 tsp cinnamon
1 cup breadcrumbs
2 tsp allspice
2 cups flour

½ tsp cloves
2 cups milk

Mix all the ingredients 3 days before baking. Then tie the mixture in a cloth dredged with flour. Lower the cloth in a pot of boiling water and boil for 5 hours. When done, drain in a colander and turn into a pudding dish. Serve with sauce.

— ⁓ —

Steamed Chocolate Pudding

1 heaped tbsp butter
1 cup sugar
½ cup sweet milk
1 egg
1 tsp cream of tartar
½ tsp vanilla
½ tsp soda
1 cup flour
2 tbsp cocoa
½ tsp salt

Mix all the ingredients together and steam for 2 hours. Serve with the following sauce:

1 egg
1 cup sugar
½ cup milk
½ tsp vanilla
a pinch of salt

Beat the egg and add the sugar and milk. Let the mixture come to a boil, stirring constantly. Serve hot.

Steamed Nut Pudding

Mrs. W. H. Scott

¼ cup butter
¹/₃ cup sugar or corn syrup
1 cup flour
1 tsp cinnamon
2 tsp baking powder
½ tsp cloves

Cream the butter and sugar or corn syrup together. Sift the dry ingredients and add to the butter mixture alternately, with ½ cup water. Add 1 well-beaten egg and a cup of finely chopped walnuts. Cook in 6 small pans or in a loaf tin. Steam for ½ an hour. Serve with hot sauce.

Steamed Pudding

Mrs. M. Fawcett

1 cup flour
½ cup sugar
2 eggs
¼ cup butter
1 tsp vanilla
½ cup milk (if sour add ¼ tsp soda)

Mix the flour with 3 tsp cocoa and 1 tsp baking powder. Add raisins, if desired. Mix in the usual way. Steam in a covered bowl for 1 hour. Serve with lemon sauce or plain thin custard.

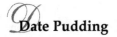

Date Pudding

Mrs. Whitfield

1 cup date, chopped
1 cup walnuts, chopped
1 cup sugar
3 eggs
3 tbsp flour
1 tsp baking powder

Mix all the ingredients together. Bake in a moderate oven for 30 minutes. Serve warm or cold with whipped cream.

Pie Plant Cobbler

R. C. Newton

Cut up 2 lb pie plant after washing well. Put them into a deep pie dish and sprinkle 1 cup sugar and ½ cup flour over it. Add, on top, a crust made as follows:

1 cup cream
1 cup flour
1 egg
1 tsp baking powder
1 tbsp sugar

Mix all the ingredients well and spread this crust over the pie plant, leaving an open space in the middle for the gas to escape. Bake well until the pie plant is tender.

Angel Date Pudding

R. C. Newton

1 cup dates, finely cut
2 tbsp flour
1 cup walnuts, chopped
2 tbsp sugar
2 eggs, well beaten
2 tsp baking powder

Mix all the ingredients well and pour this mixture into a well-buttered tin. Bake for 30 minutes. Serve with whipped cream.

Bread Pudding

Veda B. Harrah

2 cups milk
2 tbsp sugar
1 tbsp butter
1 egg
1 cup breadcrumbs
¾ tsp nutmeg or cinnamon
raisins

Heat the milk, add the sugar and butter. Stir well and pour this slowly over the beaten egg. Add the breadcrumbs, nutmeg or cinnamon and raisins. Bake in a moderate oven for 30 minutes, keeping the tin covered for the first 15 minutes. Serve with a thick sauce.

Chocolate Bread Pudding

Mrs. E. C. Lochlin

¾ cup stale breadcrumbs
2 cups scaled milk
1 oz bitter chocolate or 3 tbsp cocoa
⅓ cup sugar
⅛ tsp salt
½ tsp vanilla
1 egg, beaten

Soak the breadcrumbs in 1¾ cups milk for ½ an hour. Melt the chocolate over a pan of hot water. Stir in the sugar and the remaining ¼ cup milk and make a smooth paste. Add the chocolate to the breadcrumb mixture with salt, vanilla and egg. Pour the mixture in a well-buttered pudding dish and bake for ½ an hour till set. Serve with cream or vanilla sauce.

Rice Pudding without Eggs

½ cup rice
2 qt milk
½ cup seeded raisins
½ tsp salt
⅔ cup sugar
grated nutmeg

Wash the rice and soak in boiling water. Drain the rice and add to the milk with the other ingredients and heat the mixture till it comes to a boil. Remove from the flame and bake slowly, covered, for about 1 hour, stirring 3 times in between. Remove the cover and bake for another 2 hours to a nice brown.

Nut Pudding

1 cup molasses
1 cup suet, chopped
1 cup sweet milk
2½ cups flour
1 cup raisins
½ lb figs
2 cups walnut, chopped
1 tsp soda
a pinch of salt

Mix all the ingredients and steam for 2 hours.

Marshmallow Pudding a la Stanley

½ lb marshmallows, chopped
1 cup heavy cream
2 tbsp sugar
½ tsp vanilla
1 tbsp cherry syrup
¼ cup maraschino cherries, cut in pieces
½ cup walnuts, chopped

Whip the cream, add the sugar and vanilla and fold in the remaining ingredients. Pour the mixture into a mould and let it stand for 2 hours or till firm.

Baked Apples or Green Mango Dumplings

Mrs. Donald

4 cups flour
8 tsp baking powder
1 cup butter
1½ cups milk

Cook the apples or green mangoes with sugar to taste till half done. Sift the flour and baking powder together. Mix in the butter. Add sufficient milk to make a stiff paste. Roll them out to ¼" thick discs. Put several pieces of apple or mango into each disc and fold into a ball. Bake in the following syrup.

3 cups water
1 cup sugar
1 tbsp butter

Mix all the ingredients and let it come to a boil. Pour this syrup over the dumplings and bake in a hot oven. Serve with the following sauce:

1½ cups water
½ cup sugar
1 tbsp butter
a little nutmeg, grated
1 tsp cornflour

Mix all the ingredients (except cornflour) and bring to a boil. Thicken the mixture by adding cornflour.

Walnut Pudding

1 cup powdered sugar
1 cup dates, chopped
1 cup walnuts, chopped
4 eggs (beat whites separately)
2 tbsp baking powder

Mix all the ingredients and bake in a large tin. Serve with whipped cream.

Raisin Pudding

E. Kaufman

1 cup brown sugar
1 cup sour milk
1 egg
1 tsp vanilla
2 tbsp butter
1 cup raisins
1 tsp soda

Combine all the ingredients together and add enough flour to make a stiff batter. Steam for 1 to 1½ hours. Serve with the following vanilla sauce:

1 cup sugar
1 tbsp butter
2 tbsp flour
vanilla

Mix all the ingredients and cook until the butter melts. Add 1 cup boiling water. Flavour with vanilla. This pudding can be served with any sauce.

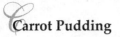

Carrot Pudding　　　　　　　　Basler Kochbuch

1 lb carrots
1 lb eggs, separated
1 lb fine sugar
1 lb almonds
½ tsp soda
1 tsp vanilla

Beat the egg yolks with the sugar. Grind the carrots and almonds in the meat grinder. Mix all the ingredients and last of all, fold in the well-beaten egg whites. Bake in a buttered baking dish to a nice brown.

Serve with custard sauce.

Graham Cracker Pudding　　　　　　Mrs. Shaw

1 cup graham crackers, rolled very fine
1 cup sugar
salt
1 tsp baking powder
½ cup walnuts, chopped
3 eggs, separated, beaten

Mix all the ingredients (except the egg whites) in the order given. Fold in the beaten egg whites, and pour the mixture in a buttered pie dish and bake in a moderate oven for 30 minutes.

Serve with whipped cream.

Crumb Pudding

1½ cups flour
½ cup sugar
½ cup butter
salt
1½ tsp baking powder
a little milk
½ cup breadcrumbs

Mix the flour, sugar, butter, salt, baking powder and a little milk to make a stiff batter. Pour the mixture into a pie dish and spread the breadcrumbs on top and bake quickly. Serve slightly hot with any sauce desired.

Scrap Bread Pudding   Mrs. Riddle

1 lb bread, slices
3 oz sugar
3 oz raisins or sultanas
3 oz currants
3 oz suet
1 oz peel, chopped
1 tsp ginger
½ tsp cinnamon
1 tsp mixed spice
dash of pepper
1 tsp soda
a little milk
1 egg

Soak the slices of bread in cold water. Squeeze them dry and crumble with a fork. Add all the dry ingredients and the soda mixed in a little milk. Fold in the egg. Steam the mixture for 2½ to 3 hours or bake in a hot oven for 45 minutes.

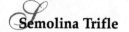

Semolina Trifle

Mrs. J. L. Gray

2 oz semolina
1 pt water
4 oz sugar
1 lemon
a little salt
chopped walnuts

Mix the semolina with water and bring it to a boil. Add the sugar. Stir and boil for 10 minutes. Remove from the flame and pour in the lemon juice and salt. Beat hard for 15 minutes or until it turns all white and frothy. Pour the mixture into a dish and set aside. Spread a layer of raspberry jam. Cover with whipped cream and decorate with walnuts.

Sago Coffee Pudding

½ cup sago
3 tbsp coffee
3 tbsp sugar
a pinch of salt
vanilla

Mix all the ingredients together and cook for about 15 minutes. Pour the mixture into a mould and serve with thick cream.

Baked Tapioca Pudding

2¼ tbsp tapioca, soaked in water for 2 or 3 hours

Boil the tapioca in 2 cups of milk. Add the butter, size of a walnut, and sugar to taste. When the mixture cools, add 2 eggs and a little nutmeg. Bake for about ½ an hour. Serve with creamy milk and sugar or a lump of butter and sugar or plain.

Baked Lemon Pudding

1 cup sugar
1 tbsp butter
2 tbsp flour
1 lemon, juice and grated rind
2 eggs, separated
1 cup milk

Mix all the ingredients, but add the stiffly-beaten egg whites last. Bake in a dish set in a pan of hot water.

Lemon Pudding   Mrs. Riddle

1 cup sugar
1 tbsp butter
2 eggs, separated
1 tbsp flour
1 cup milk
juice of 1 medium-sized lemon

Beat the sugar, butter and egg yolks together. Add the flour and milk mixed with lemon juice. Lastly, fold in the stiffly-beaten egg whites and pour the mixture into a dish. Place this dish in a pan of hot water and bake slowly.

Strawberry Shortcake

3 cups flour
2 tsp baking powder
½ tsp salt
½ cup butter
1 cup cold water
1 egg

Sift the flour, baking powder and salt together. Cut in the butter with a knife then work in with the fingertips. Beat the egg lightly and pour in the water. Add this slowly to the flour and mix well. Spread this mixture evenly in two shallow tins and sprinkle each with 2 tbsp sugar. Bake for 10-15 minutes in a very hot oven. Mash and sweeten ½ the strawberries and spread between the layers. Spread the whole strawberries on the top. Sprinkle with sugar. Pour whipped cream over the top, if desired. Hill berries taste better instead of strawberries.

Eggless Strawberry Shortcake   Mrs. Strickler

2 cups flour
4 tsp baking powder
½ tsp salt
4 tbsp butter

¾ to 1 cup milk
1 tbsp sugar

Sift all the dry ingredients together. Add the butter and milk. Work with fingertips rapidly and as little as possible. Place on a floured bread board and roll the dough into a thin round, then cut with a biscuit cutter. Place two biscuits together spreading butter between them. Bake in a greased pan and when done split each biscuit, put fresh berries which have been crushed and sweetened on the lower piece. Lay over it the top piece and cover with more berries. The dish is prettier if a few berries on the top are left whole.

Top with whipped cream, if desired.

Brown Betty

Mrs. Strickler

apples to fill a baking dish
breadcrumbs
1 cup sugar
cream
butter
cinnamon

Mix the breadcrumbs with a little sugar, cream, butter and cinnamon. Spread a layer of this mixture and then a layer of apple, sugar then breadcrumbs and so on until the dish is heaped up. Top with the crumb layer. Bake slowly till a beautiful brown on top. The bake should be a little moist, but not too dry.

Boiled Sponge and Apple Pudding

2 oz butter
4 oz flour
2 oz sugar
1 tsp baking powder
1 egg
apples
½ rind of lemon, grated

Rub the butter into the flour. Add the sugar, baking powder and well-beaten egg. Line a buttered mould with sliced apples flavoured with grated lemon rind. Cover with the flour mixture. Seal the mould with butter paper and steam for 2 hours.

Serve with custard sauce.

Gingerbread Pudding

2 oz butter
1 lb flour
1 tsp ginger
1 tsp soda
½ lb treacle
½ pt milk

Rub the butter into the flour. Stir in ginger, soda, treacle and milk. Beat well. Pour the mixture into a pan lined with butter paper. Seal the pan with butter paper and steam for 2 hours. Serve with custard or cornflour sauce.

Newark Pudding

Mrs. Hansen

1 pt milk
1 cup soft breadcrumbs
1 tbsp butter
3 eggs, separated
1 cup sugar
1 lemon, rind, grated

Boil the milk. Add the breadcrumbs and butter. When cool, add the well-beaten egg yolks with ½ the sugar, and then the grated lemon rind. Turn the mixture into a dish and bake for 15-20 minutes.

Cover with the meringue (made of the egg whites, remainder of sugar and the lemon juice). Bake till it browns slightly and serve at once without any sauce.

Chocolate Roll

2 egg, separated
2 heaped tsp sugar
2 heaped tsp cocoa
vanilla

Beat the egg yolks and sugar together until well creamed. Add the cocoa and enough vanilla to flavour. Lastly, add the stiffly-beaten egg whites. Pour in a shallow pan and bake for 30 minutes.

When cool, spread sweetened whipped cream over it. Roll as you would a jelly roll, spreading more whipped cream with each rolling. Add more whipped cream and place in a cool place.

Tomato Jelly

Mrs. Nugent

1½ cups tomato juice
1 tsp cloves
1 tsp salt and pepper
2 tsp sugar
1 packet gelatin
¾ cup cold water

Combine the first four ingredients and bring the mixture to a boil. Dissolve the gelatin in cold water and add to the tomato juice mixture. Pour in individual moulds.

❧

Pear Perfection

Mrs. Zoerner

1 tin pears
3 egg whites
1 cup granulated sugar
1 tsp vinegar
1 tsp vanilla

Fill the baking dish with pears and add a meringue made as follows: beat the egg whites gradually, adding 1 cup granulated sugar. Beat until very stiff (about 10 minutes); add vinegar and vanilla. Cook slowly until the mixture sets then bake till brown.

❧

Caramel Pudding

Dr. G. E. Miller

4 tbsp white sugar
½ cup brown sugar
1 pt milk

2 tbsp cornflour
a pinch of salt
vanilla
nuts and raisins, if desired

Melt both the sugars and stir till brown. Pour in the milk and let the mixture simmer. Add the cornflour and salt and stir till thick. Remove from the fire. Add vanilla, nuts and raisins, if desired. When cool put in the refrigerator to set.

❧

Cherry Whip

E. L. Moody

Dissolve a cherry jello packet in 1 pt of hot water. When cold, but not yet congealed, whip to the consistency of whipped cream. Pour into a glass and serve with whipped cream or custard sauce with a cherry on top.

❧

Apricot Soufflé

2 tbsp butter
4 tbsp flour
1/3 cup sugar
a pinch of salt
1 cup scalded milk
3 eggs, separated
½ tsp vanilla

Melt the butter, add the flour, sugar, salt and stir in the scalded milk. Bring the mixture to a boil. Beat the egg yolks until thick and lemon coloured and then pour the hot mixture over them, stirring constantly to prevent the eggs from curdling. Beat the egg whites till stiff, fold into the mixture and add the vanilla. Place the apricots without the juice in the buttered baking dish. Pour the mixture over them and bake for 45 to 60 minutes in a hot oven. Serve with the apricot syrup and, if desired, whipped cream.

Tapioca is another stand by in most homes. This offers variety in the way of fruit, coconut, etc., and if the minute tapioca is used, then the soufflé can be made very quickly.

━━◆━━

Plain Sauce

1 cup butter
1 cup powdered sugar

Cream the butter and sugar, then add 1 tsp vanilla. When thoroughly creamed, break in 2 eggs and beat vigorously until smooth.

━━◆━━

Lemon Sauce

1 tbsp cornflour
$1/_3$ cup butter
1 cup sugar
2 cups water
1 egg
½ lemon, sliced

Cook the cornflour, butter, sugar and water together. Remove from the fire, add the well-beaten egg and lemon slices.

━━◆━━

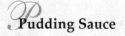

Pudding Sauce

R. C. Newton

1 tbsp flour
1 tbsp butter
½ cup sugar

Mix all the ingredients mentioned, juice of ½ a lemon and enough boiling water to make a thick sauce.

Cocoa Sauce

E. L. Moody

2 tsp butter
4 tsp cocoa
2 tbsp flour
1 cup water, hot
4 tbsp sugar
1 tsp vanilla
a pinch of salt

Melt the butter. Mix the cocoa and flour and stir into the butter. Add the hot water, gradually, and stir constantly. Just before serving, mix in sugar, vanilla and a pinch of salt.

Brown Sugar Sauce for Pudding

Stir 1 large cup brown sugar with ½ cup softened butter till creamy. Add ½ cup milk, gradually, and a few drops of cinnamon extract. Set this dish in a pan of hot water and stir. This sauce goes well with gingerbread or steamed puddings.

Everyday Sauce
Mrs. J. V. Fleming

1 pt boiling water
1 cup sugar
1 tbsp butter
1 tbsp cornflour
vanilla
a pinch of salt

Combine all the ingredients and cook thoroughly till thick.

Caramel Sauce

1 tbsp butter
½ cup sugar
a pinch of salt

Combine all the ingredients and cook till brown. Then add 1½ pt water and bring the mixture to a boil. Add 1 tbsp cornflour and cook till thick.

Ice Cream
E. L. Moody

2 eggs, separated
1 tbsp cornflour
1 cup sugar
¼ tsp salt
3 pt milk
2 seers cream
1 tsp vanilla

Combine all the ingredients (except the egg whites and vanilla). Boil and cool. Add the vanilla and beaten egg whites and cream the mixture, at the time of freezing.

For chocolate ice cream, add ½ cup cocoa and ¼ cup more sugar. Flour may be substituted for cornflour.

―◦―

Ice Cream (½ gallon)   Mrs. H. E. Wylie

1 tbsp flour
1 cup sugar
1 egg
$1/_8$ tsp salt
2 cups scalded milk
1 qt thin cream

Mix the flour, sugar, salt and lightly beaten egg. Add the milk and cream gradually and cook for 20 minutes in a double boiler. Let it cool and freeze.

―◦―

Mango Ice Cream   R. C. Newton

1 seer milk
1 cup mango, green, boiled and strained
1 cup sugar

Mix the milk with the mango pulp when cold. Then mix in the sugar and freeze.

―◦―

Pineapple Ice Cream

N. G. Alexander

1 pt water
1 pt sugar
juice of 2 limes
grated rind of 1 lime
1 small can pineapple
2 egg whites

Boil the water and sugar for a few minutes. When cool, add the lime juice, rind and chopped pineapple and pineapple juice. Freeze the mixture. When nearly frozen, add the well-beaten egg whites.

Note: The limes are the ordinary small *nimbu*. The eggs are *desi* eggs.

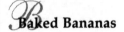

Baked Bananas

Mrs. Bauman

Take 1 large or 3 small bananas for each person to be served. Peel the skins and cut into strips, lengthwise. Keep the sliced bananas in a lightly buttered dish. Pour over them the following mixture:

2 tbsp brown or white sugar
1 tbsp lemon or lime juice
1 tbsp water

Bake in a moderate hot oven for 15 minutes. Serve at once. This mixture is enough to bake the bananas for 4 people.

Banana Fritters or Pancakes Mrs. Burgoyne

¼ cup flour
1 tbsp sugar
a pinch salt
1½ tsp baking powder
1 egg, beaten
½ cup milk
1 tsp butter, melted
2 large bananas, mashed

Mix all the ingredients into a smooth batter. Heat the oil in a pan; add 1 tbsp of batter and fry till golden brown on both sides. Repeat till all the batter is used up.

Serve hot with lemon sauce or jelly.

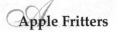

Apple Fritters Mrs. M. R. Long

10 or 12 sour apples
1 cup flour
2 tsp baking powder
a pinch of salt
3 eggs

Pare and core the apples. Cut the apples in ½" slices. Mix the remaining ingredients, adding enough milk to make a thin batter. Dip the slices of apple into the batter completely covering them, and fry in deep fat. Serve hot.

Apples Stuffed with Dates   Gladys Holmes

6 medium apples
6 dates

Core the apples. Remove the pits from the dates and chop finely. Fill the apples with the date pulp and bake in a moderate oven. Dust the apples with the grated coconut and sprinkle sugar when cold. Serve with cream.

—◆—

Blushing Apples   E. W. Ross

Poor apples may be used for this dish, as they will be finely flavoured and pretty. Mellow apples will not do. Peel and core as many apples as you have people to serve. For 6 good sized ones, put 1 cup white sugar and 2 cups water to boil, adding 2 tbsp little red hot candies (cinnamon drops). When this begins to boil, drop in the apples and boil them till tender, but not till they drop to pieces. Then turn them over so that they are red on all sides. Put the apples into individual dishes, boil the juice until it jellies and pour it over them.

Serve with whipped or plain cream although neither is really needed.

—◆—

Green Ginger   Gladys Holmes

Soak and clean the ginger well. To each pound of ginger allow 1½ pt water. Boil it down to 1 pt or even less. Skim it carefully when boiling. Strain off the liquid and add 1 lb sugar candy and boil till the ginger is tender.

Poached Peaches

B. Kaufman

Spread half a canned peach on a slice of cake, make a ring of meringue around the peach. Brown in the oven. Pour custard around the cake. Place a few chopped walnuts on the custard and serve.

~

Ambrosia

Mrs. P. A. Friesen

Take 6 oranges and 6 bananas. Peel and slice, then arrange in a dish a layer of oranges sprinkled with sugar. Then a layer of bananas, sprinkled with coconut, and so on till the dish is full. Serve with cream or sauce.

~

Confectionery

You have asked me to write you of cake,
Of puddings and tartlets and pies
Do you know what a time it would take,
For such a dull dullard as I?
We eat what we find on the board
And thankful we are, if there's any
But recipes, I've a great hoard
And gladly will send you a many.
But as for the tried and the true
The tested and always OK.
I must leave the decision to you
For every good cook likes her way.

M. H. R

CAKES

Making Cakes at High Altitudes

An ordinary cake recipe is liable to be a failure at an altitude of 5,000 ft or higher, but it can be easily modified to give perfect results at any of the higher levels at which it may be used. It has been found that in almost every instance the sugar is the deciding factor for the success of a cake recipe used at a high altitude. As the elevation increases, the proportion of sugar to use decreases, and always in a given proportion. The same general rule applies to cookies or to any flour mixture in recipes which have a higher percentage of sugar than flour. It is especially true of drop cookie mixtures, or of other thin doughs, but even the mixtures to be rolled, such as plain sugar cookies, need to be proportioned in this way.

Adjustments for Cakes at High Altitudes

Baking temperature: At all altitudes over 3,500 ft increase the baking temperature by 25°F.

Flour: At 3,500 ft add 1 tbsp flour per recipe and then add 1 tbsp more for each 1,500 ft increase in elevation above 3,500.

Eggs: Use maximum amount of eggs called for in the recipe. If part of the egg is needed to make a full measure, add the egg white, not the egg yolk.

Sugar: For every 2,500 ft of elevation, reduce each cup of sugar called for in the recipe by 2 tbsp, starting to estimate the change at 2,500 ft. The three standard recipes tabulated (see p. 131) may be adapted for use at various altitudes by modifying the sugar content as directed in the table.

Adjustments of Sugar Measurements at Various Levels:

Sea Level to 2,500 ft
Plain Cake 1½ cups
Rich Cake 1½ cups
Drop Cookies ½ cup
Plus 2 tbsp

2,500 to 5,000 ft
Plain Cake 1 cup
Plus 5 tbsp
Rich Cake 1½ cups
Drop Cookies ½ cup
Plus 1 tbsp

5,000 to 7,500 ft
Plain Cake 1 cup
Plus 2 tbsp
Rice Cake 1½ cups
Drop Cookies ½ cup

By Anna L. Steckleberg

Wherever asterisk (*) is used follow this method of mixing and baking.

Rules for Mixing and Baking Cakes
1. Have everything at hand before beginning.
2. Work the butter till creamy.
3. Add the sugar gradually.
4. The egg yolks should be thoroughly beaten (or until thick).
5. Beat the egg whites till stiff and dry.
6. Add the milk and flour alternately (having sifted the salt and baking powder with the flour).
7. Fold in the egg whites last.
8. Bake in a moderate oven.

Never Fail Cake  Margaret Mumby

½ cup butter
1 cup sugar
3 small eggs or 2 large ones
½ to ¾ cup milk
2 cups flour
2 heaped tsp baking powder
1 tsp vanilla

Cream the butter and sugar together. Add the beaten eggs and mix. Add the milk and flour sifted with baking powder and salt, alternately. Add the vanilla. Bake in a moderate oven.

Icing for Never Fail Cake
Cook 1½ cups sugar and ½ cup water until it threads. Beat the whites of 2 eggs until very light. Pour the syrup over the egg whites slowly. Beat until creamy. Pour over the cake and sprinkle with grated coconut.

Good Plain Cake Miss Burgess

3 cups flour
2½ tsp baking powder
½ tsp salt
¾ cup butter
1½ cups sugar
4 eggs
¾ cups water
flavouring

Sift the flour, baking powder and salt 3 times. Cream the butter and sugar. Break in one egg, mix well. Add a little flour and water. Beat well. Continue till you have used all the eggs, flour and water. Add the flavouring last. Bake in a moderate oven.

❦

Plain Cake

G. E. Springer

2 cups sugar
½ cup butter
4 eggs
½ cup milk
2½ cups flour
2 heaped tsp baking powder

This is a cake that can be used as a foundation recipe, and can be made all white, yellow or changed in various ways. When made in the hills, reduce the sugar to 1½ cups.

❦

Marble Cake*

White Part
4 egg yolks
1 tsp cloves
1 cup brown sugar
1 tsp cinnamon
¼ cup butter
1 tsp nutmeg
½ cup sour milk
½ tsp soda
1 tbsp syrup
1 cup flour

Dark Part
4 egg whites
1 cup sugar
½ cup milk
½ cup butter
1 tsp cream of tartar or
2 tsp baking powder
½ tsp soda
1 tsp lemon
1½ cups flour

See page 131 for rules. Alternately put spoonfuls of both the mixtures in a loaf pan. Bake in a moderate oven till done.

—❦—

Checkerboard Cake
E. L. Moody

4 squares bitter chocolate
(cocoa may be used)
1 cup fat
1 cup sugar
4 cups flour
6 tsp baking powder
½ tsp salt
1½ cups milk
1 tsp vanilla
6 eggs, separated

Cream the fat and add the sugar gradually. Sift the flour and baking powder together, add to the fat mixture alternately with milk. Stir in vanilla and the beaten egg whites. Divide the batter into 2, mix the chocolate in one-half. Arrange the plain and chocolate batter into 6 alternate stripes. Bake in a moderate oven at 350°F. Cool and put together the similar coloured stripes on the top and the bottom layers while a different one in the centre. Cover with white icing.

Cake for the Hills*

E. F. Chambers

½ cup sugar
½ cup butter
2 cups flour
2 tsp baking powder
1 cup milk
3 egg whites
flavouring

See page 131 for rules.

Bread Dough Cake*

M. L. Picken

1 cup sugar
1 tsp soda in 1 tbsp water
½ cup butter
1 cup raisins
1 egg
1 cup yeast
1½ cups flour
1 tsp cinnamon
1 tsp allspice

Let the batter stand for about 45 minutes and bake for about
an hour. See page 131 for rules.

Eggless Cake

M. H. R.

1 cup brown sugar
½ cup shortening

1 cup sour milk
½ tsp baking powder
3 cups flour
½ cup white sugar
½ tsp salt
½ tsp nutmeg
½ tsp cinnamon
1 cup raisins or currants
1 tsp soda

Cream together the sugar and shortening. Add the sour milk and the dry ingredients. Bake for 15-30 minutes in a hot oven.

Sunshine Cake

E. L. Moody

3 less egg yolks than it takes to fill a cup of whites
1 cup egg whites
¼ tsp cream of tartar
1 cup sugar
1 cup flour
1 tsp orange flavour

Beat the egg yolks till very light. Add the cream of tartar to the egg whites and beat till stiff. Fold the yolks into the whites. Then add the sugar, flour and orange flavour.
Bake in an ungreased pan for 45 minutes. To remove the cake from the pan, run a knife around the edge, and loosen the bottom with a knife or fingers. Turn it upside down on a plate and dredge with white icing.

Golden Cake

M. L. Clark

2½ cups flour
½ tsp soda
2 heaped tsp baking powder
8 egg yolks or 4 whole eggs
1 tsp cream of tartar
½ cup butter
1½ cups sugar
1 tsp lemon extract
½ cup sweet milk

Sift the flour, soda and baking powder thrice together. Beat the eggs and add the cream of tartar when half beaten. Cream the sugar and butter together. Add the eggs and the lemon extract, then the milk and flour mixture. Beat well and bake in a loaf tin. Nuts or candied peel can be added, if desired.

Gold Cake

Miss Drummond

1½ cups sugar
½ cup water
6 eggs, beaten separately
¼ tsp salt
1 cup flour
¼ tsp cream of tartar
1 tsp orange extract

Boil the sugar and water till it threads. Pour this hot syrup over the beaten egg whites to which salt has been added. Beat the mixture till stiff. Then add the egg yolks. Sift the flour and cream of tartar. Fold in the flour mixture and mix.

Icing: 1 cup white icing sugar mixed with grated rind and juice of 1 orange.

White Cake

Mrs. Strickler

1½ cups granulated sugar
½ cups butter
1 cup milk
3 cups flour
5 egg whites
vanilla
2 tsp baking powder

Cream the sugar and butter well. Alternately, add milk and flour and do not let the mixture curdle. Fold in the egg whites. Lastly, add the vanilla and baking powder with a fork.

Silver Cake*

M. M. Saum

7 egg whites
½ cup milk
2 cups powdered sugar
2 tsp baking powder
½ cup butter
1 tsp vanilla

Bake in a loaf tin for ½ an hour. See page 131 for rules.

Caramel Cake

M. M. Saum

2 cups sugar
6 small eggs (save 2 whites for icing)
½ cup butter

1 cup milk
3 cups flour
2 tsp baking powder
1 tsp vanilla

To make caramel, heat ½ cup sugar in a pan until it dissolves and is brown in colour. Remove from the fire and cool a little. Pour enough water to make a syrup. Add to the cake batter before mixing in the flour.

— ❧ —

Burnt Caramel Cake

1½ cups sugar
½ cup butter
2 eggs, separated
1 cup cold water
3 cups flour
1 tsp baking powder
1 tsp soda
1 tsp vanilla
3 tbsp burnt caramel

To make burnt caramel, put ½ cup sugar in a skillet and cook till brown. Add 1 cup boiling water and cook till the mixture is as thick as syrup. Let it cool. To make the cake batter, cream the butter and sugar and add the egg yolks, then the water. Beat in the flour to which baking powder and soda have been added and sifted several times. Now add 3 tbsp of burnt caramel and vanilla and beat till light. Fold in the stiffly-beaten egg whites and bake.

To make the icing, boil 2 cups sugar and 1 cup cream in the skillet where burnt caramel was made, until it forms a soft ball, or use any caramel icing.

Banana Cake Baked in Loaf

Mrs. Strickler

1 cup sugar
½ cup butter
2 cups flour
½ tsp baking powder
¼ tsp salt
¾ tsp soda
¼ cup sour milk
2 eggs, separated
1 tsp vanilla
1 cup bananas, mashed

Mix like any other cake, adding the bananas and the stiffly-beaten egg whites in the end. Bananas should be ripe. This cake is always moist.

Boston Favourite Cake*

Elma Hill

½ cup butter
2 cups sugar
4 eggs, lightly beaten
3½ cups flour
½ tsp salt
5 tsp baking powder

Cream the butter and gradually add the sugar and eggs. Mix in the dry sifted ingredients and add a little milk. See page 131 for rules.

Quick Cake

Elma Hill

½ cup butter
1½ cups flour
1½ cups brown sugar
3 tsp baking powder
2 eggs
½ tsp cinnamon and nutmeg
½ cup milk
½ lb dates, finely cut

Mix all the ingredients in a bowl and beat for 3 minutes. Bake for 35 to 40 minutes.

Note: If the ingredients are added separately, this cake will fail.

Chocolate Cake

Mrs. Strickler

½ cup butter
1½ cups sugar
2 eggs
4 tbsp cocoa
½ cup boiling water
½ cup thick sour cream
1½ cups flour
¼ tsp soda
1 tsp vanilla

Cream the butter and sugar. Add the eggs, beaten separately. Melt the cocoa with boiling water, add sour cream and flour (sifted 3 times with soda). Beat well and add vanilla. Cook in a medium oven. This cake may be served hot with sweetened whipped cream.

Devil's Food Cake

Hope Nicholson

1 cup brown sugar ⎤
½ cup sweet milk ⎥ First part
1 cup chocolate, grated ⎥
1 cup butter ⎦

Combine all the ingredients and bring it to a boil. Cool and mix with the second part. Flavour with vanilla.

1 cup brown sugar ⎤
½ cup butter ⎥
½ cup sweet milk ⎥ Second part
3 eggs yolks ⎥
2 cups flour ⎥
2 tsp baking powder ⎦

Filling
1 cup sugar
1 tbsp cornflour
1 egg
1 cup milk

Boil all the ingredients for the filling and when cool add a small bit of butter, 1 tsp vanilla and ½ cup chopped walnuts. Spread the filling between the layers and over the top.

Cocoa Cake*

Mrs. Beuleh

1 cup sugar
4 tbsp butter, melted
1 egg
1 tsp salt

1 tsp soda
¼ cup or less, cocoa

Mix into a thin batter and bake. See page 131 for rules.

Fudge Cake
Mrs. D. O. Cunningham

1½ oz sugar
¼ cup butter
2 egg yolks
½ cup sweet milk
¼ slab of chocolate, melted or
5 tbsp cocoa dissolved in 5 tbsp hot water
1¾ cups flour

Cream the sugar and butter, add the well-beaten egg yolks, milk, melted chocolate or cocoa and flour. After stirring well, add 1½ tsp baking powder and well-beaten egg whites.

A Good Cake
Mrs. Zoerner

1 cup sugar
2 cups flour
1 egg
5 tbsp cocoa
1 cup sour milk
1 tsp soda
5 tbsp shortening
¾ cup raisins
¾ cup walnuts

Mix all the dry ingredients, add egg, cocoa dissolved in about ½ cup hot water, milk, soda and shortening. Beat well. Add the raisins and walnuts. (If nuts are used 3 tbsp shortening will suffice.)

— ❧ —

Fruit Cake

1 cup butter
2 cups raisins
2 cups sugar
1 cup currants
1 cup syrup (molasses can be used)
1 cup walnuts
1½ cups sour milk
1 cup candied peel
5 eggs
1 tsp cinnamon
5 cups flour
a pinch of allspice, cloves, nutmeg

Mix all the ingredients and bake for 2 hours. You can make one large or two small cakes.

— ❧ —

English Fruit Cake

2 cups butter
2 cups sugar
10 eggs, beaten one at a time

Beat the butter and sugar to a soft cream. Mix in 5 heaped cups of flour with 1 tbsp allspice and 1 tsp salt. A little of this may be added as each egg is beaten in. Add:

> 2 cups currants
> 1 cup milk
> 1 cup candied peel
> 2 cups raisins
> 1½ cups almonds, blanched, chopped
> ½ cup preserved cherries
> grated rind of 2 lemons

Bake for 5 hours.

Wacky Crazy Cake
Larry Smith and D. Bunce

> 1½ cups flour
> 1 cup sugar
> 3 tbsp cocoa
> 1 tsp salt
> 1 egg, well beaten
> 1 tsp soda
> 1 tbsp vinegar
> 5 tbsp shortening, melted
> 1 tsp vanilla
> 1 cup water

The wacky thing about this recipe is that if you use a large cake pan, you can mix and sift the first four ingredients in the pan itself!

Make 5 holes in the mixture and place one of the next 5 ingredients in each hole. Pour water over the top and mix well (use a fork). Bake at 350°F for 25 minutes.

Almond Fruit Cake

Mrs. D. T. Miller

¾ lb sugar
¾ lb butter
½ pt eggs (6 or 7)
¾ lb flour, sifted
¼ lb almonds, ground
1 lb raisins, sultanas and currants
6 oz peel and citron, chopped
1 cup walnuts, chopped

Cream the sugar and butter well. Alternate, between eggs and sifted flour. Then add the almonds and lastly, the floured fruit and nuts. Bake slowly for 3½ hours.

Note: This will keep well for weeks. The almonds make the cake moist and provide a good flavour.

Blackberry Jam Cake

E. L. Moody

2 cups sugar
1 cup butter
4 eggs
1 cup sour milk
1 tsp soda
3 cups flour
1 tsp cinnamon
1 tsp cloves
1 tsp allspice
1 tsp nutmeg
2 cups raisins
1 cup blackberry jam
2 tbsp cocoa

Cream the butter and sugar. Beat the eggs in, one at a time. Add the milk mixed with soda, flour mixed with spices and cocoa, jam and raisins. Some spices may be omitted. Bake in layers or in 2 loaves. In a loaf tin, bake for about 1½ hours.

Mother's Cake

Miss Helm

1 cup butter
1½ cups sugar
3 eggs, separated
½ cup milk
3 cups flour
3 tsp baking powder
a pinch of salt
1 tsp vanilla
½ cup currants
½ cup dates, chopped fine and floured
1 cup walnuts, finely chopped

Cream the butter. Add the sugar, gradually, then the egg yolks. Add the milk, flour, baking powder, salt and vanilla. Lastly add the currants, dates and walnuts.

Walnut Cake

½ cup butter
1 cup sugar
3 egg yolks
½ cup milk
2½ tsp baking powder
1¾ cups flour

½ tsp salt
2 egg whites
¾ cup walnuts

Put the cake batter into a tube cake pan lined with paper.
Bake in a moderate oven for 45 minutes.

❧

Maple Nut Cake

Mrs. Howard

½ cup shortening
2 tsp baking powder
2 egg yolks
1 cup nuts
½ cup light brown sugar
1 tsp vanilla
¾ cup milk
1½ cups flour
½ tsp salt

Icing
½ tsp butter
2 tbsp hot milk
1½ cups icing sugar
½ tsp maple, flavouring

Boil together all the ingredients of the icing and spread over
the cake.

❧

Three-egg Butter Cake

Frankline Presler

¾ cup shortening
1½ cups sugar
3 eggs, well beaten
1 tsp vanilla
3 cups flour
2½ tsp baking powder
¾ tsp salt
1 cup milk

Mix like any other cake. Bake in a greased 8″ pan at 375°F for 20-25 minutes.

Angel Food Cake

Mrs. Zoerner

1 cup egg whites
¾ tsp cream of tartar
1¼ cups granulated sugar
¾ tsp vanilla
1 cup flour (sifted 4-7 times)
¼ tsp salt

Beat the egg whites until foamy, not stiff. Add the cream of tartar gradually. Fold in the sugar, 1 spoonful at a time. Add the flavouring and fold in the flour mixed with salt, gradually. Do not beat as other cake batter. Pour in an ungreased pan and bake in a slow oven for 50 to 60 minutes.

Brown Sponge

D. Mathew

3 oz butter
¼ lb sugar
3 eggs
¼ lb flour
1 tbsp cocoa
½ tsp soda
1 tsp cream of tartar
vanilla flavouring

Beat the butter and sugar till creamy. Beat the eggs separately and add to the butter mixture. Mix in the flour and other ingredients. Bake for 20 minutes in a moderate oven.

Cream filling
1 tbsp butter
1 tbsp sugar
1 tbsp hot water (not boiling)
vanilla flavouring

Beat all the ingredients together until it becomes creamy. Slit the cake horizontally and spread the cream filling between the 2 layers.

Sponge Cake

Mrs. B. Lucas

4 eggs
1½ cups sugar
2 cups flour
2 tsp baking powder
¼ tsp salt
1 cup boiling water
1 tsp lemon essence or lemon juice

Beat the eggs till very light. Then mix in the sugar and flour which has been sifted with salt and baking powder, a little at a time. Add the boiling water, gradually, then the flavouring. Put the mixture into a large ungreased tin and bake in a slow oven for 1 hour.

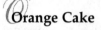 **Orange Cake** O. B. Dodds

½ cup butter
1½ cups sugar
4 egg yolks
¾ cup orange juice and grated rind of orange
½ cup cornflour
4 tsp baking powder

Icing
2 cups icing sugar
1 tbsp butter
3 tbsp orange juice
a little grated rind of orange

Mix and bake like any other cake.

 Tea Cake A. B. Cowdry

2 eggs, separated
1 cup sugar
1 heaped tbsp butter
2 cups flour
2 tsp baking powder
½ cup milk

Cream the egg yolks, sugar and butter together. Sift the baking powder with the flour. Fold in the flour and egg whites, beaten stiffly, alternately. Bake in a moderate oven. Excellent eaten with Lemon Cheese

Lemon Cheese
6 eggs
the juice of 4 good-sized lemons
and the grated rind of 3

Heat the sugar, lemon juice and the grated rind together. Stir till the sugar dissolves. Pour into the beaten eggs, beating all the while. Cook over a pan of boiling water until it thickens, stirring continuously.

Coffee Cake

Merle T. Rice

2 tbsp butter
$^1/_3$ cup sugar
2 eggs, separated
3 cups flour (after sifting)
2 tsp baking powder
a pinch of salt
$^1/_3$ cup milk

Cream the butter and sugar, add the egg yolks, flour sifted with baking powder and salt, and milk, alternately. Lastly add the egg whites. Pour the batter in a baking tin. Sprinkle ½ cup walnuts and ½ cup raisins over the batter. Then sprinkle some sugar and a pinch of cinnamon. Bake for 30 minutes in a moderate oven. Spread with butter if desired, after removing from the oven.

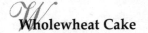

Wholewheat Cake

Kittu Riddle

½ cup butter or margarine
1 cup brown sugar
2 eggs
2 cups *atta* (wholewheat atta), sifted
1 tsp baking powder
½ tsp salt
1 tsp soda
1 cup sour milk
1 tsp vanilla

Mix and bake like any other cake. Pour the batter into 2 well-oiled layer cake tins and bake at 350°F for 25-30 minutes.

❧

Layer Cake

M. Manry

butter, size of a walnut
2 cups sugar
1 egg
1 cup flour
1 tsp baking powder
½ cup milk
vanilla

Cream the butter. And the sugar, beaten egg, flour mixed with baking powder, milk and vanilla. Mix well and bake.

❧

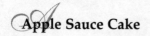pple Sauce Cake

Mrs. A. L. Miller

½ cup butter
1 cup sugar
2 cups flour
²/₃ cup raisins
allspice to taste
1 cup sweetened apple sauce
into which ½ tsp soda is added

Cream the butter and sugar. Make the batter a day before using. Bake in a loaf tin.

Upside Down Cake

Miss Drummond

4 tbsp butter
4 tbsp brown sugar
1 small can crushed pineapple, drained
1 cup walnuts

Cake batter
3 eggs, separated
4 tbsp shortening
1 cup sugar
½ tsp salt
1½ cups flour
2 tsp baking powder
½ cup milk or cream

Beat the egg whites till stiff. Mix the cake batter in the usual way. Then prepare the first four ingredient as follows: melt the butter in a pan. Stir in the brown sugar. Then pour this mixture over the pineapple and add the walnuts. Pour the cake batter over this and bake for 45 minutes. When done, turn the cake upside down and serve with whipped cream.

Ice Cream Cake

5 egg whites, well beaten
2 cups sugar
1 cup butter
1 cup milk
3 cups flour
3 tsp baking powder

Bake in layers.

Icing for ice cream cake
Boil together 2½ cups sugar and ½ cup water. Beat the whites of 3 eggs. When the syrup threads, pour it into the egg whites and stir as quickly as possible. Flavour with vanilla and spread over the cake.

❦

Sour Cream Cake

R. C. Newton

Break 1 egg into a cup and fill the cup with sour cream. Pour this mixture into a mixing bowl and beat well with an egg beater, gradually adding 1 cup sugar, 1¾ cups flour mixed with 1 tsp soda and a pinch of salt. Flavour and bake.
Makes 12 nice party cakes.

❦

Ginger Cake

1 cup brown sugar
½ cup lard and butter mixed
1 cup molasses

1 cup buttermilk
2 eggs
1 tsp cinnamon
1½ tsp ginger (more if desired)
2 tsp soda
a little nutmeg
2½ cups flour

Mix and bake like any other cake. Splendid.

Gingerbread Damp

Mrs. J. L. Gray

6 oz butter
6 oz sugar
10 oz flour
¾ tsp soda
1½ tsp cinnamon
4 oz sultanas
3 oz almonds
3 oz preserved ginger
1½ tsp ground ginger
¼ lb treacle
2 eggs
warm milk

Cream the butter and sugar. Add all the dry ingredients and treacle. Then the well-beaten eggs and a little milk, if necessary. Bake in a moderate oven for 2 hours.

Dutch Gingerbread

Mrs. Cornuelle

Wash and dry 1lb currants and mix with 4 cups flour.

1 cup butter, creamed
1½ cups sugar
1½ cups molasses
4 eggs
½ cup sour milk
1 tsp soda
1 nutmeg, grated
1 tbsp ginger
1 tbsp cinnamon

Mix and bake like any other cake.

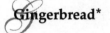

Gingerbread*

Mrs. Strickler

¼ cup butter
¼ cup sugar
1 tsp soda
½ cup molasses
½ cup water
1 egg
1 tsp cinnamon, cloves and ginger
1¼ cups flour
currants

Add the flour and currants last. Make a thin batter. Bake slowly in a medium oven. See page 131 for rules.

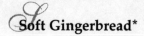

Soft Gingerbread*

2 eggs
1 cup butter or shortening
1 cup sugar
1 cup molasses
1 pt buttermilk
1 tbsp soda
1 tsp cinnamon
1 tbsp soda
1 tsp cloves

See page 131 for rules.

❧

Spice Cake*

1 cup sugar
$^2/_3$ cup butter
3 eggs or 6 yolks
1 tsp soda
1 cup sour milk
2½ cups flour
1 cup raisins
1 cup carrots
1 tsp cloves
1 tsp cinnamon
1 tsp salt
1 tsp allspice

Mix the sugar, butter and eggs. Beat well. Stir the soda in the milk and add the flour and the remaining ingredients. Mix well. Bake in a loaf tin. When done, dredge with white icing. See page 131 for rules.

Cinnamon Cake*

D. Mathew

1 cup sugar
1 tbsp butter
1 egg
1 cup sour milk
1½ cups flour, sifted with 1 tsp soda
and 1 tbsp cinnamon

Mix in the order given. Enough for two layers. See page 131 for rules.

Chiffon Cake

Maxine Burch

2¼ cups flour
1½ cups sugar, fine
3 tsp baking powder
1 tsp salt
½ cup salad oil
7 egg yolks
¾ cup cold water
3 tbsp vanilla or grated orange rind
2 tsp lemon extract
1 cup egg whites
½ tsp cream of tartar

Sift together the first 4 ingredients. Make a well and add the next 5. Beat the egg whites with cream of tartar until stiff. Pour the egg yolk mixture gradually over the egg whites, gently folding in until blended. Pour the batter into an ungreased tin and bake at 325°F for 55 minutes. Then increase the temperature to 350°F and bake for 15 minutes more or till the top springs back when slightly touched.

ICINGS

Plain Icing

1 egg
3 tbsp milk
2 tbsp butter
1 cup sugar
2 tbsp cocoa

Beat the egg, add milk, butter, sugar and cocoa. Cook slowly over a low flame, stirring constantly.

When the mixture comes to a boil, remove from the fire, add vanilla and beat until thick enough to spread. This comes out just right if directions are followed.

Vienna Frosting

Miss L. Clark

¾ lb icing sugar
1 lb butter
¼ lb chocolate, finely powdered

Mix all the ingredients together for about 15 minutes. Add a few drops, at a time, of orange juice till light and creamy.

Cake Frosting

1 egg white, unbeaten
1 cup sugar
3 tbsp cold water

Mix all the ingredients in a double boiler. Cook for 6 to 7 minutes. Remove, and when almost cool add:

1 tbsp corn syrup
1 tsp baking powder
3 tsp flavouring
marshmallows

Beat all the ingredients and then add the marshmallows.

Caramel Icing

¾ cup sugar
¼ cup water
2 egg whites
½ tsp baking powder
1 tsp vanilla

Heat the sugar and water in a saucepan. Stir until the sugar dissolves. Boil until it spins a long thread. Add this syrup, gradually, to the well-beaten egg whites. Add the baking powder and vanilla, and beat until stiff.

Chocolate Icing
Mrs. Zoerner

2 tbsp butter
2 cups powdered sugar
2 squares melted bitter chocolate
6 tbsp cold coffee (hot coffee may be used)
¼ tsp salt
½ tsp vanilla

Cream the butter with the sugar. Add the melted chocolate, coffee and salt, stir until thick. Then add vanilla and (if hot coffee is used) keep aside to cool. When cold, spread this over the cake. This icing may be used any time. It is just as good made a day before and used the next by adding a little more hot coffee. It is always soft, creamy and delicious.

❦

Icing for Chocolate Cake

1 tbsp butter
1½ cups icing sugar

Combine the two ingredients and add milk or cream to make it soft enough to spread. Beat this very well till it is fluffy.

❦

Cake Frosting

R. C. Newton

¾ cup brown sugar
¾ cup white sugar
3 tbsp water
2 egg whites

Boil the sugar and water until it spins a thread and then add rapidly to the beaten egg whites.

❦

COOKIES

*S*ugar Cookies with Filling

Mrs. E. C. Lochlin

½ cup butter
1 cup sugar
2 eggs
¼ cup milk
2 cups flour
2 tsp baking powder
¼ tsp vanilla or any other flavouring

Cream the butter and sugar. Fold in the beaten eggs mixed with milk. Sift 1 cup flour with baking powder and add to the butter mixture with the the rest of the flour. Roll on a floured board ¼" thick. Cut with a biscuit cutter. Bake in a hot oven at 375°F for 8 to 10 minutes.

Filling: Mix the flour and sugar, boil together until thick. Before baking the sugar cookies, place 1 tsp of this filling on the lower half of the rounds and cover with another round, pinching the edges well together.

*P*rize Sugar Cookies

Mrs. Donald

2 cups sugar
1 cup butter
3 eggs
½ cup milk
1 tsp soda
2 tsp cream of tartar
a pinch of salt
flour to roll

Cream the butter and sugar. Add the beaten eggs and milk.
Add flour mixed with soda, cream of tartar and salt. Roll out,
cut and bake.

Cream Cookies

M. M. Saum

2 cups sugar
1 tsp lemon extract (or ½ grated nutmeg)
1 cup sour cream
2 eggs
1 cup butter
1 tsp soda

Combine all the ingredients and add enough flour to make a
soft dough that can be rolled out. Cut and bake.

Delicate and Crisp Cookies

Mrs. M. Fawcett

12 oz flour
3 tsp baking powder
¼ lb butter
4 eggs
3 tbsp milk
9 oz sugar
a pinch of salt
lemon essence

Mix all the ingredients and roll. Handle lightly, adding
enough flour to keep it from sticking. Roll out, cut and bake
in a hot oven at 450 to 500°F.

Imperial Cookies

E. F. Chambers

½ cup butter
1 cup sugar
2 eggs
1 tbsp milk
2½ cups flour
2 tsp baking powder

Mix all the ingredients and add lemon, vanilla or nutmeg. Roll out a thin dough. Cut and bake.

❦

Spice Cookies

Neva Nicholson

1 cup molasses
½ cup sugar
9 tbsp milk
1 egg
4 cups flour
1 tsp soda
1 tsp each cinnamon, nutmeg, cloves, salt

Bring the molasses to a boil. Add the sugar, milk and egg. Mix and sift the dry ingredients, add to the milk mixture. Chill, then roll out and cut. Bake in a moderate oven.

❦

Cinnamon Cookies

Mrs. Hansen

1 cup sugar
1 egg
1 cup molasses

1 cup shortening
1 tbsp vinegar
salt
1 tbsp cinnamon
1 tbsp soda (½ in molasses, ½ in flour)

Mix all the ingredients and add enough flour to make a stiff dough. Roll out a thin dough. Cut and bake.

~

Ginger Wafers

Miss Burgess

1 cup each sugar, butter and treacle
1 tbsp ginger
1 tsp cinnamon, cloves and nutmeg
1 tsp soda dissolved in a little water

Cook the butter, treacle and sugar with the spices in a saucepan. When it begins to boil, remove and add the soda. While foaming, stir in enough flour to make a very stiff dough. Roll out a thin dough. Cut with a 2" diameter cutter. Bake in a moderate oven. When cold, pack in a tin box. No other cake or cookie can be put in the box with them. This makes at least 12, 2" diameter wafers.

■

Molasses Ginger Cookies

Mrs. Whitfield

½ cup butter
1 cup molasses
1 tsp each soda and cinnamon
1 tbsp ginger

Cream the butter and mix it with the molasses. Sift a cup of flour with the soda and cinnamon and add. Add more flour to make a soft dough that can be rolled out.

Roll out a thin dough and sprinkle with granulated sugar. Gently press the sugar into the dough with a rolling pin. Cut out and bake for about 10 minutes in a hot oven.

———

Molasses Cookies with Coconut

1 cup molasses
½ cup boiling water
1 cup sugar
1 cup shortening
1 tbsp soda, ginger, cinnamon and nutmeg

Mix all the ingredients and add enough flour to make a very stiff dough. Roll out, cut and bake.

Icing   Mrs. Cornuelle
1 packet clear gelatin
1 pt cold water
1 cup sugar
a pinch of salt

Soak the gelatin in water till it dissolves. Add the sugar and boil till the mixture is stiff. Remove from the fire and beat hard, adding flavouring. Before it cools completely, pour on the cookies and cover with grated coconut.

———

Good Ginger Cookies

Mr. Ebey

1 cup molasses
1 tbsp ginger
1 cup sugar
½ cup coffee (already made)
1 cup shortening

Dissolve 2 tsp soda in the coffee. Mix all the ingredients together. Stir in the coffee mixture and add enough flour to roll out a medium thick dough. Cut and bake in a hot oven.

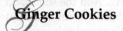

Rochester Ginger Snaps

1 cup molasses
1 cup sugar
1 cup butter

Mix all the ingredients and boil for 5 to 8 minutes. Let the mixture cool and then add 1 tsp each of cinnamon, ginger and soda. Add enough flour to roll out a very thin dough. Cut and bake in a hot oven.

Ginger Cookies

Mrs. Rugg

8 cups flour
2 cups molasses
1 cup sugar
½ cup hot water
2 or 3 eggs
2 small tsp soda

1 cup of lard
1 tbsp ginger

Place the flour in a large bowl and add the other ingredients.
Mix and keep the dough overnight.

❧

Suji Cookies

E. L. Moody

½ cup butter
1½ cups flour
2 eggs
¼ cup *suji* (semolina)
¼ cup sugar
1 tsp cinnamon
¼ tsp salt
½ cup raisins
3 tsp baking powder

Mix all the ingredients. This makes 3 dozens 2 by 2½″
cookies.

❧

Oatmeal Biscuits

M. R. Long

1 cup sugar
½ cup flour
1½ cups rolled oats
a little salt

Mix all the ingredients. Roll out a thin dough. Cut and bake.

❧

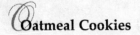 Oatmeal Cookies

R. C. Newton

                2 cups sugar
                2 cups flour
                2 cups oatmeal
                1 cup shortening
                1 tsp salt
                1 tsp cloves
                2 tsp cinnamon
                1 tsp nutmeg
                3 eggs, well beaten
                1 cup walnuts
                1 cup raisins
                1 tsp soda

Mix all the ingredients together. It is difficult to mix, but worth the trouble. Shape into balls and set apart on buttered tins to bake.

Cream may be used instead of the shortening. If the raisins and walnuts are put through a meat grinder it makes it nicer for children.

Rolled Oats Cookies

M. M. Saum

                1 cup butter (½ lard if desired)
                ½ cup sour milk
                1 tsp soda
                2½ cups rolled oats
                1 cup sugar
                1 tsp salt
                2 eggs
                flavouring

Mix all the ingredients and add sufficient flour to roll.

Scottish Fancies

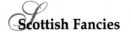

Mrs. Strickler

1 egg
½ cup sugar
1 cup rolled oats
¹/₃ tsp salt
½ tbsp butter, melted
¼ tsp vanilla

Beat the egg until light, gradually add the sugar, then stir in the remaining ingredients. Drop the mixture from a spoon on a thoroughly greased pan 1" apart. Spread into circular shape with a case knife first dipped in cold water.

Bake in a moderate oven until delicately browned. To give variety use ²/₃ cup rolled oats and ¹/₃ cup grated coconut.

Oatmeal Macaroons

Merle T. Rice

1 cup rolled oats
½ cup butter
1 cup flour
1 cup brown sugar
1 tsp baking powder
1 egg

Mix all the ingredients together and add vanilla and salt.

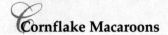

Cornflake Macaroons

Mrs. Harner

1 cup sugar
1 tsp vanilla
a pinch of salt
4 cups cornflakes
1 cup coconut, grated
1 cup walnuts, chopped
4 egg whites, beaten

Mix all the ingredients and add to the beaten egg whites. Bake in a slow oven. Makes 40 macaroons.

Coconut Macaroons

4 egg whites
1 cup fine sugar
2 cups coconut, grated
lemon juice and vanilla

Beat the egg whites and sugar in a bowl until very stiff. When well beaten, stir in the coconut and add the flavouring. Cover the baking tin with buttered paper laid out in small biscuits, pinching them together. Bake in a very slow oven for 30 minutes or until a light brown colour.

Coconut Puffs

Mrs. P. A. Friesen

1 cup coconut, grated
½ tbsp flour
1½ cups powdered or fine granulated sugar
2 egg whites, beaten stiff
½ tbsp cornstarch
1 tsp baking powder
a pinch of salt

Mix all the ingredients and drop on buttered tins and bake quickly.

Date Coconut Bars

J. V. Fleming

¾ cup flour
½ tsp baking powder
salt
1 cup coconut or ½ cup chopped walnuts
1 cup dates
2 eggs
1 cup brown sugar

Mix and sift the baking powder, salt and flour. Mix in the coconut or walnuts and dates which have been pitted and cut in small pieces. Beat the eggs well and then add the brown sugar and stir in the sifted ingredients. Spread in a well-greased pan about ½" thick. Bake for 30 to 40 minutes. Cut in strips about 4" long and 1" wide.

Yum Yum

Mrs. A. E. Parker

1 cup flour
2 tsp baking powder
¼ tsp salt
2 eggs, beat whites separately
1 cup sugar
½ cup sweet milk
1 cup dates, chopped
1 cup walnuts, chopped

Sift all the dry ingredients together. Add the remaining ingredients. Bake in a greased tin for 30 minutes. Cut while hot and roll in sugar.

Date Crackers

Mrs. Roberts

1 lb dates
1 cup sugar
1 cup boiling water
1 egg
2 cups oat flakes
½ cup butter
2 cups flour
1 cup sugar
½ cup milk
½ tsp soda
1 tsp cream of tartar
1 tsp salt

Boil the dates and sugar together. Keep aside. Mix the remaining ingredients. Divide the mixture into two parts. Roll both out into the same size and shape. Spread dates on

one and cover with the other. Cut either before or after
baking.

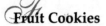ruit Cookies

2 cups sugar
1 cup butter
2 cups raisins
1 cup sour milk
½ cup citron
1 cup currants
1 tsp soda
2 eggs
1 tsp each cinnamon, cloves and salt

Mix all the ingredients together. Drop into a greased pan
with a spoon.

Fruit Bars   Mrs. Bradley

3 eggs (beat 1 cup sugar with the yolks)
1 cup flour
1 cup walnuts, broken
½ tsp salt
1 cup dates, ground
1 tsp baking powder
2 tsp vanilla

Fold in the beaten egg whites last. Spread thinly and bake.
Cut into strips and roll in sugar as soon as it is baked, as they
harden when cold.

Fig Cookies

1 cup butter
1 cup brown sugar
4 tsp cream of tartar
4 eggs
2 tsp soda
3 cups flour
½ cup *atta* (wholewheat flour)
½ tsp salt
1 tsp vanilla

Make a dough, roll and spread with fig jam. Fold and cut.

━━━━━

Robins

Miss Drummond

2 egg whites, beaten
1 cup walnuts, chopped
½ cup white sugar
1½ cups cornflakes
1 cup dates, chopped

Drop on a buttered tin and bake.

━━━━━

Filled Cookies

Mrs. Livengood

1 cup sugar
1 egg
½ cup butter
1 tsp soda
½ cup sweet milk
1 tsp cream of tartar

3 cups flour
1 tsp vanilla

Mix together like a cake and when stiff enough to handle then roll out and cut. Spread a tsp of the filling on one cookie, pressing the edges down. Bake.

Filling
1 cup raisins, chopped
½ cup water
½ cup sugar
1 tsp flour

Cook together until a soft wax is formed.

May Cakes

Mrs. Griswold

2 eggs, separated
1 cup sugar
¼ cup butter
1½ cups flour
1 tsp cinnamon
½ tsp cloves and nutmeg
1 tsp soda
½ cup sour milk
½ cup molasses
½ cup raisins
1 cup walnuts

Beat the egg yolks and, gradually, stir in the sugar, butter, flour and the spices. Dissolve the soda in 1 tbsp of boiling water and add the sour milk and molasses. Add this to the egg mixture. Fold in the well-beaten egg whites, raisins and walnuts. Bake in small gem pans.

Brownies

Mrs. A. E. Parker

½ cup cocoa
½ cup butter, melted
3 eggs
1 tsp baking powder
1 cup sugar
½ tsp salt
½ cup flour
1 cup walnuts, chopped
1 tsp vanilla

Add the cocoa to the melted butter. Mix in the remaining ingredients. Spread thinly on buttered sheets and bake for 12 minutes.

Chocolate Nut Cookies

Mrs. D. T. Miller

1 cup shortening
1 cup sugar
2 eggs
½ cup cocoa
1 cup walnuts, finely chopped
1 tsp vanilla
3 cups flour
1 tsp baking powder
1 tsp salt
½ tsp soda

Cream the sugar and shortening. Add the eggs, cocoa, walnuts and vanilla. Gradually add the sifted flour, baking powder, salt and soda. Knead into 2 rolls and let them chill overnight. Cut into thin discs and bake.

Indians

Mrs. Shaw

> 2 squares of chocolate (or 8 tbsp cocoa)
> ½ cup butter
> 1 cup sugar
> 2 eggs, beaten
> ¾ cup flour
> 1 cup walnuts
> vanilla

Melt the chocolate and butter together. Mix the sugar and eggs and add the chocolate mixture, flour, walnuts and vanilla. Bake in a moderate oven and cut in squares while still warm.

Cocoa Cakes

> 2 egg whites
> 1 cup sugar
> 1 tsp vanilla
> 1 tsp salt
> 1 cup dried breadcrumbs
> ¼ cup cocoa

Beat the egg whites, add sugar and vanilla, salt, breadcrumbs and cocoa. Pour the mixture into a greased tin and bake in a moderate oven for 20 minutes.

Hermits

6 tbsp shortening
1 cup brown sugar
1 egg
½ cup milk
1½ cups flour
2 tsp baking powder
¼ tsp salt
1 tsp cloves
1 tsp allspice
1 tsp cinnamon
1 cup seeded raisins, chopped
2 tbsp citron, chopped

Cream the shortening, add the brown sugar and beaten egg. Mix well. Add the milk gradually. Sift the flour, baking powder, salt and spices together and add slowly to the sugar mixture. Add the fruits dredged with flour.

Pour the mixture into a greased tin and bake in a moderate oven for 15 minutes.

Brown Sugar Drop Cake

2 cups brown sugar
½ cup butter
2 eggs
1 tsp soda in ²/₃ cup sour milk
vanilla
½ cup raisins
½ cup walnuts

Mix all the ingredients together and add enough flour to make a stiff batter.

Drop from a tsp into a tin and bake, or else, bake in a very thin sheet and cut into squares later.

Peanut Drop Cakes

Mrs. Shaw

2 tbsp butter
¼ cup sugar
1 egg
½ cup flour
¼ tsp salt
1 tsp baking powder
2 tbsp milk
½ cup peanuts, finely chopped
½ tsp lemon juice

Cream the butter, add sugar and the well-beaten egg. Sift the flour, salt and baking powder and mix with the butter mixture.

Then add the milk, peanuts and lemon juice. Drop from a tsp on an ungreased sheet 1" apart. Bake in a moderate oven for 12 to 15 minutes. Makes 24 cookies.

Aunt Cathie's Cookies

Miss Helm

1 cup lard and butter mixed
2 cups sugar
3 eggs
¾ pt sour cream
1½ tsp soda
3 cups flour
1½ tsp baking powder

Beat the lard and butter with sugar and eggs well. Add the sour cream and the dry ingredients. Mix till soft. Bake in a moderate oven.

Lemon Crackers

E. L. Moody

3 cups sugar
2 eggs
1 pt lard
1 pt sweet milk
8 tsp carbonate of ammonia
1 tsp oil
lemon
3 qt flour

Roll out, cut with a square cutter, prick with a fork and bake in a hot oven.

Graham Crackers

1 cup flour
1 cup graham flour, or *atta* (wholewheat flour)
a pinch of salt
½ cup sugar
2 tsp baking powder
½ cup butter
2 eggs

Add enough water so that it can be rolled out like cookies. Cut in any desired shape. Prick with a fork before baking.

Cake without Milk

3 eggs
1½ cups sugar
1 cup lard and butter mixed
2 tsp cream of tartar
lemon or vanilla flavour
1 tsp soda

Mix all the ingredients and add enough flour to make a stiff batter. Roll out a thin dough, cut and bake in a hot oven.

DOUGHNUTS

Whoever invented the doughnut
Should in no wile be counted a 'slow nut'
For no one has yet solved the riddle
Of the funny round hole in the middle.

Let the optimist highly delighted
View the doughnut as a rich toothsome whole,
Let the pessimist deeply benighted
See nothing else here but the hole,
As for me, if I'm clever and bright,
I shall eat the whole 'sab chiz' outright.

Dr. J. H. Orbison

—◆—

Doughnuts

Miss Burgess

3 cups flour
2 tsp baking powder
½ tsp salt
1 tbsp butter, melted
1 cup sugar
2 eggs

Sift the flour, baking powder and salt thoroughly. Mix the butter, sugar and egg together till smooth. Add the flavour of your choice. Then add the flour mixture with enough sweet milk to make a dough stiff enough to be easily handled without sticking. Roll out and cut in rings and fry till golden brown in a deep wok containing smoking hot fat.

The doughnuts may be sprinkled with sugar as soon as they are taken out from the wok.

Drop or Puff Ball Doughnuts

2 cups flour
2 tbsp baking powder
¼ tsp salt
nutmeg
½ cup sugar
2 eggs
1 tbsp butter
½ cup milk

Mix all the ingredients together. Take ½ tsp of this batter and drop into hot fat. Cook until brown. Drain on absorbent towels.

❦

Georgia Doughnuts

Myrtle Furman

2 eggs
1 cup sugar
½ tsp soda
1 cup sour milk
2 cups flour
½ tsp nutmeg
3 tsp baking powder
½ tsp salt

Beat the eggs till very light, then add in the sugar. Mix the soda in the sour milk and add to the egg mixture. Lastly, add the flour sifted with nutmeg, baking powder and salt. Add more flour to roll. Cut and fry in hot oil and turn each doughnut as it rises to the surface. To make these with sweet milk, follow the same method, but omit the soda.

Afternoon Tea Doughnuts

Mrs. Whitfield

2 eggs
6 tbsp sugar
¼ tsp salt
¼ tsp nutmeg, grated
2 tbsp shortening, melted
6 tbsp milk
2 cups flour
3 tsp baking powder

Beat the eggs until very light. Add the sugar, salt, nutmeg, shortening and milk. Add the flour and baking powder that have been sifted together. Mix well. Drop 1 tsp of batter into the hot fat and fry till brown. Drain well on unglazed paper and sprinkle with powdered sugar.

━━━

Good Doughnuts

2 eggs
1 cup sugar
1 tsp salt
½ tsp nutmeg
1 heaped tsp lard
1 cup sour milk
1 tsp soda

Mix all the ingredients and add enough flour to make a very soft dough. Fry in smoking hot fat.

━━━

Potato Doughnuts

2 medium-sized potatoes, mashed
2 tsp lard
1 egg
½ cup milk
1½ cups sugar
4 tsp baking powder
½ cup flour

Mix all the ingredients and add enough flour to make a stiff dough. Fry like any other doughnut.

***

Mother's Doughnuts   Mrs. A. L. Miller

1½ cups sugar
2 tbsp butter, melted
2 eggs, well beaten
1 tsp cinnamon
1 tsp salt
a little nutmeg
1 tsp soda in 2 tbsp hot water
1 cup milk

Mix all the ingredients well and add enough flour to make a soft dough. Fry like any other doughnut.

***

Snow Balls
Mrs. P. A. Friesen

2 eggs
½ cup sugar
1 cup sweet milk
2 tbsp baking powder
a little salt and flavouring

Mix all the ingredients and add enough flour so that they drop from a spoon. Fry in hot deep fat like doughnuts and sprinkle with powdered sugar. These taste as good as doughnuts and are easier to make.

Kentucky Chocolate Crullers
E. L. Moody

3 tbsp shortening
2 eggs
1¼ cups sugar
½ tsp soda
1 cup thick sour cream
1 tsp vanilla
1 tsp cinnamon
5 cups flour
3 tsp baking powder

Mix all the ingredients and roll ¼" thick. Cut as doughnuts or shape in figure 8 and fry in deep fat.

PASTRIES AND PIES

Mince Pie

Lovely mince pie, dreamland pastry!
Thoughts of spicy island fill me –
Summer seas with languorous breezes
Filtering through the moonbeams still me.
Wond'rous mince pie, nectar dripping!
Crusted dream of pure delight!
Eat your own and be contented,
For of mine there's not a bite!

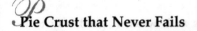

Pie Crust that Never Fails   R. C. Newton

1 cup shortening, chopped into pieces
1 cold water
2 cups flour
1 tsp baking powder
1 tsp salt

Mix the shortening and water in a bowl. Then, gradually, stir
in the flour, salt and baking powder sifted together. Handle
the mixture as lightly as possible until it forms a ball in the
bowl then mould and use. This will make half a crust pie and
shell for an open pie.

Pastry

1 cup shortening
½ cup boiling water
3 cups flour
1 tsp salt
1 tsp baking powder

Soften the shortening in boiling water. Add the dry ingredients and mix with a spoon. Chill before using.

❦

Crust

1 cup flour
1 tbsp lard
a little salt

Mix all the ingredients with water. A good way to test whether the pie crust is short enough is to squeeze the flour in your hand after mixing in the lard; it should stick together.

❦

Puff Paste

1 cup flour
½ tsp baking powder
½ tsp salt

Sift together the ingredients 3 times. Work in about 1 tbsp butter with tips of the fingers. Add enough cold water to make a soft dough. Roll out about ¼″ thick and spread the butter all over it as you would when buttering bread rather liberally. The butter does not need to be very hard. It must spread well. Sprinkle a little flour all over the buttered paste. Fold over several times and roll out again. Spread the butter, add the flour and roll up again. Repeat this 4 times. Roll up and either use immediately or leave standing in a cool place till needed. Always cut through the folds not across them. Fold over and over, then roll and cut.

Hot Water Pie Paste

1½ cups flour (measure after sifting)
1 tsp baking powder
1 tsp salt

Sift the ingredients together. In ½ cup shortening, butter, *ghee* or lard add ¹/₈ cup boiling water. Stir until it resembles oil. Add to the sifted flour. If not soft enough to roll out, add a little cold water. Use plenty of flour on board when rolling out.

Pie Crust for Lemon Pie

For one crust
3 oz shortening
1 cup flour
a pinch of baking powder
¼ tsp salt

Sift the flour with baking powder and salt, add the shortening. Add water gradually. Roll one way on floured board. Bake in a quick oven. When done, cool. Pour cool lemon custard filling into the crust shell. Whip 2 egg whites, spread on top and brown in the oven.

Meringue

Add 2 tbsp cold water to 4 stiffly-beaten egg whites. Add 4 tbsp sugar and beat. Fold on top of the pies and brown in the oven.

Lemon Pie

Mrs. Shaw

1 lemon rind and juice
4 tbsp water
4 tbsp sugar
4 eggs yolks

Combine all the ingredients and cook slowly until thick. Cool and add 2 egg whites beaten with 2 tbsp sugar. Use the other 2 egg whites for the meringue.

Lemon Pie

4 tbsp cornflour, dissolved in a little cold water
1 cup boiling water
1 tbsp butter
salt
juice and grated rind of 1 lemon
1 cup sugar
2 egg yolks

Combine all the ingredients and cook till thick. Fill into a crust. Use egg whites for meringue. If the eggs are small use three.

❧

Tennessee Angel Lemon

M. M. Saum

3 eggs, separated
¼ cup lemon juice
½ tsp salt
1 cup sugar
grated rind of ½ lemon

Beat the egg yolks until thick. Add the other ingredients and half the sugar. Cook in a double boiler until very thick, stirring constantly. Cool. Beat the egg whites till stiff and dry. Add the remaining sugar, then fold into the egg mixture. Fill into a baked crust. Brown in a moderate oven for 15 minutes.

❧

Lemon Chiffon Pie

O. B. Dodds

2 egg yolks
½ cup sugar
juice and grated rind of lemon (3 or 4 limes)

Mix and cook all the ingredients slowly, stirring constantly. Beat the egg whites till very stiff and add ½ cup sugar. Mix this with the above custard. Fill into a baked crust and brown slightly.

❧

Cream Pie

Mrs. Donald

Roll the puff paste till very thin. Line a pie plate with this puff paste and bake in a hot oven.

Filling
2 cups milk
2 tbsp cornflour
1 tbsp sugar

Mix all together and cook, stirring constantly. Cook for 5 to 10 minutes. Pour while still hot into a baked crust after adding some vanilla. Beat the egg whites till stiff and add 2 tbsp sugar and a few drops of vanilla. Fold in the egg white mixture over the milk mixture. Sprinkle some freshly grated coconut. This taste better when not browned in the oven.

━━●━━

Jeff Davis' Pie

Yolks of 2 eggs, a lump of butter, 1 cup brown sugar, 1 tsp vanilla, 2 tbsp flour, 1 cup water or milk. Use whites for meringue. Mix like any other pie.

━━●━━

Coconut Cream Pie

Elma Hill

1 pt milk
½ cup sugar
2 egg yolks
1 tbsp flour
1 tsp lemon extract

Mix all the ingredients and add coconut, if desired. Beat the egg whites and spread on top. Brown slightly.

Date Cream Pie

Merle T. Rice

4 tbsp butter
4 tbsp flour
½ tsp salt
2 cups milk
½ cup sugar
1 cup dates, pitted and cut in pieces
2 eggs

Melt the butter. Add the flour and salt. Stir in the milk and cook until it thickens. Then add the sugar. Stir in the dates which have been cooked in a very small amount of water. Add the well-beaten eggs. Pour into a lined pie tin and bake until brown.

Sour Cream Date Pie

Mrs. A. E. Parker

1 egg
1 cup sugar
1 tsp flour
1 cup sour cream
¼ tsp salt
1 cup dates, chopped

Beat the egg. Add the sugar and flour. Add the sour cream, salt and dates. Bake in a pie crust with cross strips of crust over it.

Sour Cream Pie 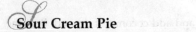 R. C. Newton

Make an ordinary pie crust and line a pie tin, then add 1 cup raisins. Line the crust with this custard.

For the custard
1 cup sour cream
1 cup sugar
1 tbsp flour
2 egg yolks

Mix all the ingredients. Pour this custard over the raisins and bake. When done, it will puff up in the middle a bit. Make a meringue of egg whites and brown. Delicious, but rich.

Raisin Pie

2 cups raisins
1½ cups water
½ to 1 cup sugar
½ tsp salt
2 tbsp lemon juice
2 tbsp cornflour, mixed with a little cold water
1 tbsp butter

Boil the raisins in water till tender. Add the other ingredients. Fill a double crusted pie and bake.

Chocolate Pie

½ cup sugar
1½ tbsp flour
1 tbsp cocoa
1 cup milk
2 eggs, separated
salt

Cook the sugar, flour and cocoa together. Add the milk and beaten egg yolks. Pour the mixture into a baked crust and cover with the egg whites beaten stiff with 2 tbsp sugar. Brown in the oven.

Pie Filling

Mrs. Cornuelle

½ cup brown sugar
grated rind of 1 lemon
1 cup molasses
2 cups water
½ tsp salt
5 tbsp flour
2 tbsp butter

Cook all the ingredients for 5 minutes. Pour into a pastry-lined pie dish, cover with strips of pastry. Bake until the filling is thick.

Mince Meat Pie

7 cups dried apples, cooked, mashed
2 cups carrots, ground, if desired
2 cups suet, raw
½ cup candied peel
3 cups lean beef, cooked, ground
4-5 cups sugar
2 tbsp salt
2 cups large raisins, seeded, cut
1 tbsp allspice
1 tbsp cloves
2 cups rose juice and sifted pulp
(can substitute mangoes or any tart fruit)
2 tbsp cinnamon

Boil all the ingredients together until well cooked and seal the mixture in airtight jars till ready to use. At the time of baking, add walnuts and apples. Bake in double crusts.

❦

Mock Mince Meat

2 cups stale breadcrumbs
¼ cup vinegar
3 eggs
¾ cup water
1 cup treacle
1 cup sugar
1 tsp each cloves, nutmeg and cinnamon
butter, size of a walnut
½ tsp salt

Cook the above mixture, then pour in a baked crust. This preparation is delicious. One can hardly tell from real mince meat.

Fresh Fruit Pie

Mrs. E. C. Lochlin

Roll out a thin pastry ¼" thick. Bake on an inverted tin. When cool, fill with 1 qt strawberries or any other fresh fruits like pineapple, orange, banana, apricots, peaches or pears. Sprinkle with sugar. Cover with boiled frosting (as for cake) and brown slightly or with whipped cream sweetened and flavoured. The flavour of the fruit is improved if it has been allowed to stand for several hours on ice after being sweetened.

Dried Apple Pie

Soak, cook and mash the dried apples. Sweeten to taste. Add cinnamon or nutmeg. Fill into a double crust and bake like a fresh fruit pie.

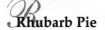Rhubarb Pie

M. M. Saum

1 cup rhubarb, stewed
2 egg yolks
1 cup sugar
2 tbsp flour

Cook all the ingredients and pour in a baked crust. Use the egg whites for the meringue.

Squash Pie

Line a pie tin with ordinary crust, then fill with:
1 cup squash, cooked, strained
1 tbsp butter, melted
½ cup sugar
1 tsp ginger
1½ cups milk
1 tsp cinnamon
1 tbsp molasses
a pinch of salt
1 egg

Mix all the ingredients well and bake in the crust. The pie is done when a knife inserted in the centre comes out clean.

Syrup Tarts   Miss Drummond

¼ cup brown or white sugar
$1/_3$ cup water
butter, size of a walnut

Mix all the ingredients and bring it to a boil. In a separate bowl mix:

½ cup sugar
1 egg
a pinch of salt
½ tsp flavouring

Mix all the ingredients thoroughly and pour it into a pie crust. Bake in a moderate oven.

Green Tomato Pie

Mrs. A. E. Parker

4 medium green tomatoes, thinly sliced
½ lemon, thinly sliced
½ tsp cinnamon
½ tsp salt
1½ tsp cornflour
1 tsp butter

Cook the tomatoes and lemon with cinnamon and salt till tender. Then add cornflour and cook until thick. Add the butter and mix well. Pour the mixture in a crust. Cover with a top crust and bake.

Sweet Potato Pie

1 pt sweet potato pulp, boiled
1 pt milk
1 cup sugar
a pinch of salt
2 egg yolks
a little lemon juice or extract
2 egg whites
1 tbsp powdered sugar

Mix the sweet potato pulp, milk, sugar, salt, egg yolks and lemon juice together. Stiffly beat the egg whites with the powdered sugar. Mix with the milk mixture and pour over a shallow-lined crust. Bake till brown.

CANDY

I'm the sweetest thing in the book by right,
I put the others far out of sight
I travel much, I cross the seas
I go to many fancy teas;
In my delicate colours and striped attire
I'm much admired by all of Landour
I'm boiled and pulled and hard to beat
I'm no cheap guy I am a first class treat
It's here an anna and there a dime
I'm eagerly sought for in every clime.

If all the foods were soups and meat,
Or even rare fried froggies' feet
Who'd bother very much to eat –
Would you?
But if you top a meal with fudge,
Sea foam or caramel. I judge
Until dessert no one will budge. It's true?

H. I.

Peanut Brittle

Merle T. Rice

1 cup corn syrup
2 cups sugar
½ cup water
1 tsp butter
2 cups peanuts, roasted
½ tsp vanilla
2 tsp soda

Cook the corn syrup, sugar and water until it begins to thicken and bubble. Add the butter and peanuts. When a firm ball forms in cold water, remove from the fire, and add vanilla and soda and stir through quickly. Pour the mixture into a well-greased platter. When it flattens out, loosen it with a knife and flop it over quickly.

❧

Peanut Butter Fudge

4 cups sugar
6 tbsp corn syrup
3 tbsp cocoa
1 tsp salt
1½ cups milk

Combine all the ingredients and cook over a moderate flame until it forms a soft ball in cold water. Remove from the fire and add 3 tbsp peanut butter. Beat hard till cool and very stiff. Pour into a pan and flatten out to cut.

❧

Chocolate Fudge   Mrs. Livengood

2 oz chocolate
2 cups sugar
½ cup sour cream or sour milk
1 tbsp butter
½ tsp salt
½ tsp vanilla

When cooked and cool enough to handle, knead into a soft dough. Cut into squares.

Walnut Chocolate Caramel
Mrs. E. C. Lochlin

6 oz grated chocolate or cocoa
1 cup cream
1 cup granulated sugar
1 cup brown sugar
1 cup corn syrup
1 cup milk
1 tbsp flour
1 cup walnuts, broken
1 tsp vanilla

Stir the chocolate and cream to a smooth paste. Add both the sugars, corn syrup, milk and flour and cook over a slow fire for nearly an hour, stirring constantly till a few drops poured in cold water forms a firm chewy ball. Then add the walnuts and vanilla. Pour into a buttered pan 1" deep. When cold, mark into squares. When hard, cut with a heated knife.

❧

Chocolate Caramel
Mrs. B. C. Harrington

1 cup brown sugar
2 lb golden syrup
2 oz butter
½ cup cocoa
½ cup milk
1 tsp vanilla

Cook till the mixture forms a hard ball in water.

❧

Coconut Raisin Caramel

C. E. Pope

1 lb seedless raisins
¼ lb coconut, shredded

Mix the ingredients well and run them through a food chopper. Roll out and cut into squares.

Caramel

Vesta Miller

1 cup molasses
butter, size of a walnut
1 cup brown sugar
vanilla
1 cup cream or milk

Beat all the ingredients together. Boil till it thickens. Pour the mixture into a flat tin. When nearly cold, cut into squares.

Molasses Toffee

E. L. Moody

1 cup sugar
2 cups molasses
3 tbsp vinegar
1 tbsp butter
½ tsp soda

Boil all the ingredients together until it makes a hard ball in cold water. Pour the mixture on greased plates and cut when cool enough to handle.

African Sea Foam

M. M. Saum

1 cup milk
2 cups sugar
¼ cup vinegar
½ cup golden syrup
2 egg whites, well beaten
1 cup walnuts
vanilla

Boil the milk, sugar, vinegar and golden syrup till it forms a firm ball in cold water. Fold in the egg whites and beat. Add the walnuts and vanilla.

❧

White Taffy

Mrs. E. C. Lochlin

2 cups sugar
²/₃ cup water
4 tbsp butter
2 tsp cream of tartar
1 tsp flavouring

Mix the first four ingredients in a sauce pan and boil till a very hard ball forms, i.e., when a few drops turn brittle in cold water. Add the flavouring. Pour into a buttered pan and when cold enough to handle, mix with fingertips. Stretch on a board to harden and cut. Easy and quick to make.

❧

English Toffee

Vesta Miller

2 oz sugar
4 oz golden syrup
5 tbsp heavy cream
½ tsp salt
¼ oz butter
2 oz light brown sugar
1 oz walnut
¼ tsp vanilla

Cook the sugar, golden syrup, cream and salt till a soft ball forms, then add the butter and cook till it forms a medium hard ball. Remove from the flame, add the walnuts and vanilla. Pour into a buttered dish and when cool, cut and wrap in wax paper.

Mexican Fudge

Mrs. Strickler

3 cups sugar
1 cup milk
1 tbsp butter
1 tsp vanilla

Melt 1 cup sugar in a saucepan over a slow flame. In another saucepan, put 2 cups sugar, milk and butter. Bring the mixture to a boil then add the melted sugar. Stir constantly to keep the mixture from sticking to the bottom of the pan. Let it cook till it forms a soft ball in cold water. Remove from the fire, add the vanilla and beat.

When it begins to thicken, add 1 cup walnuts and beat until creamy.

Russian Toffee

E. W. Ross

2 cups brown sugar
2 tbsp butter

Mix the ingredients and cook till the sugar melts. Then mix in ½ pt condensed milk. Remove from the flame and stir till it cools. Let the mixture stand for a while and then cut.

Fondant

2 cups sugar
½ cup boiling water
1 tsp cream of tartar
½ tsp glycerine

Boil all the ingredients till it makes a jelly like ball in cold water. Let the mixture cool, then beat till light and creamy. Knead till smooth. This can be beaten over a bowl of hot water and used for dipping little cakes or icing large cakes, or for making Bon Bons.

Maple Fondant

Mrs. Menzies

2 cups sugar
1 cup corn syrup
1 cup water

Boil all the ingredients together until it spins a thread. Let it cool. When it begins to stiffen, beat and then knead. Mix fruits, cocoa, etc., for variety.

Cream Candy

3 cups sugar
¾ cup rich milk or cream

Boil for 5 minutes, stirring all the time. Remove from the flame, stir until cold enough to mould with the hands. Dip into melted chocolate and place on a buttered paper.

Marshmallows

M. M. Saum

2 tbsp gelatin
⁵/₈ cup cold water
2 cups sugar
⁵/₈ cup water
a pinch of salt
1 tbsp cornflour
1 tsp vanilla

Soak the gelatin in cold water. Boil the sugar in water until it threads. Pour this hot syrup over the gelatin mixture and beat with a wire egg beater. While beating, add salt, cornflour and vanilla.

Turkish Delight

Mrs. Donald

1 oz sheet gelatin
½ cup cold water
2 cups sugar
juice of 1 orange and 1 lemon

Dissolve the gelatin in cold water. Boil the sugar in ½ cup water till the sugar dissolves. Add the gelatin and boil for 20 minutes. Remove from the fire and add the fruit juice. Pour into a square pan about 1″ deep. When stiff, cut into squares and roll in icing sugar.

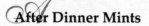After Dinner Mints

E. L. Moody

3 cups sugar
½ tbsp vinegar
¼ tsp cream of tartar
½ cup boiling water

Boil the ingredients rapidly with little stirring till it becomes brittle in cold water. Pour into buttered plates, adding 2 drops of peppermint oil. Cut in small pieces.

Nougats

Miss Vance

1 lb golden syrup
1½ lb sugar
½ pt water
2 egg whites
1 tsp vanilla
½ lb walnuts, chopped

Cook the golden syrup, sugar and water till a very hard ball forms, but is not brittle. Stiffly beat the egg whites and pour in the sugar syrup, beating constantly. Continue beating and stirring till the mixture is rather stiff and waxy looking. Then add the vanilla and walnuts. Mix well and pour into a small box or a pan lined with greased or waxed paper. Let the mixture stand overnight, then turn out and slice, as desired. This does not have to be beaten hard and fast, just keep it moving constantly.

❧ ⸻ ❧

Gulab Jamuns

Mrs. Shaw

1 seer khoa (wholemilk fudge)
1½ pao flour
1 *chattak* clarified butter

Rub all the ingredients well together. Divide the dough into balls and put half a *batasha* (sweet made with powdered sugar) in the centre of each ball and cover. Fry in hot clarified butter. Then drop into a thick hot sugar syrup.

❧ ⸻ ❧

Jalebies

2 cups lukewarm water
3 cups flour
1 tbsp cottage cheese or cornmeal
2 tbsp sour milk
2 tbsp clarified butter or lard

Mix the first 4 ingredients and let it stand overnight to rise. When ready to fry in smoking hot clarified butter, add ¼ tsp soda in the batter. Then force a stream of batter through a cloth in which you have made a tiny hole, into ringlets. Let it brown on both sides, drain and then drop into syrup.

Syrup: Make a thin syrup before you begin to fry the *jalebies*:

4 cups sugar
1 cup water
1 tbsp vinegar

Immerse the *jalebies* in the syrup for a while and then remove. These are best served soon after cooking.

Sea Foam

Miss Kerr

1½ cups sugar
¼ cup golden syrup
$^3/_8$ cup water
2 or 3 egg whites
1 cup walnuts

Heat the sugar, syrup and water till it turns brittle in cold water. Cook slowly so that it is lighter. Don't stir while cooking. Beat the egg whites till very light. Pour the syrup in the egg whites, add walnuts. If you have no walnuts, add vanilla. Put them in tin boxes to prevent them from getting soft.

Chopsticks

3 lb seeded raisins
¼ lb walnuts
¼ lb coconut, shredded

Mix all the ingredients and put them through a food chopper using a fine cutter. Roll in sticks, 4" long. Wrap in waxed paper.

Figola

1½ lb dried black figs
¼ lb dried olives, pittted
¼ lb peanuts, unroasted

Mix all the ingredients and put them through a food chopper.
Roll out and cut into squares. Wrap in waxed paper.

Fig Fudge

¼ lb figs, chopped
2 cups sugar
½ tsp ginger
1 cup cold water or milk
1 tbsp butter
¼ tsp salt

Boil all the ingredients together till it makes a ball in cold
water. Beat till creamy and pour into a buttered plate. Cut in
squares.

❧

Panouche

2½ cups sugar
½ cup syrup
2 cups cream
1 cup nuts
½ cup raisins
½ tsp vanilla

Cook the sugar, syrup and cream till it thickens. Remove from the flame and beat till very thick. Add the nuts, raisins and vanilla. Put the mixture in a damp cloth. Keeps well.

Salted Almonds

M. M. Saum

Blanch the almonds by pouring boiling water over them and rub the skins off. When dry, pour 1 tbsp melted butter over each cup. Let it stand for an hour, then sprinkle 1 tbsp salt. Mix well and brown in the oven.
Peanuts can be done in the same way.

Popcorn Calls

Cook together 1 cup sugar, 1 cup syrup, 1 tbsp vinegar and a pinch of salt till it hardens when dropped in cold water. Pour this mixture over 4 qt of popped corn and let it stand until cool enough to mould with hands. Then shape into balls.

Breads and Rolls

—◆—

THE CORN

Oh! I am a king with an endless reign,
My subjects hunger never;
For famines may come and famines may go,
But I am faithful ever.

Dr. G. E. Miller

Bread

E. L. Moody

5 cups flour
5 cups lukewarm water
2 tbsp yeast
7 cups *atta* (wholewheat flour) or refined flour
4 tbsp molasses
4 tsp salt

Mix flour, water and yeast in a large bowl. Let the mixture stand overnight. In the morning, mix in the *atta* or flour, molasses and salt. Knead the mixture well and pour it into greased pans to rise. Fill the pans till about half full. Bake for 1 hour. It can be turned after it has been in the oven for ½ an hour.

Raisin and Nut Bread

Jennie E. Crozier

2 cups graham flour
1 cup white flour
1 tsp soda
1 tsp salt
1 tsp baking powder
½ cup brown sugar
1½ cups sour milk or buttermilk

2 tbsp molasses
1 cup walnuts and raisins

Mix all the dry ingredients together. Add the brown sugar and mix well. Add the sour milk and molasses and stir until smooth. Add the walnuts and raisins and mix well. Pour the mixture into a well-greased pan and bake in a moderate oven (350°F) for 1 hour 10 minute or until done.

Southern Spoon Bread

Mrs. H. E. Wylie

1 qt milk
2 cups corn
1 tsp salt
3 tbsp fat
1 egg, separated

Heat the milk (½ water may be used). Stir in the corn, salt and fat and cook for 5 minutes. Remove from the flame and let the mixture cool. Add the beaten egg yolks first then the stiffly beaten egg whites. Pour the mixture into a greased pan and bake in a moderate oven for 40 minutes. Serve hot. This is served with pork.

Gingerbread

Miss Drummond

2½ cups flour (sift before measuring)
1 tsp soda
1 tsp baking powder
½ tsp salt
2 tsp ginger
1 tsp cinnamon
1 cup sour milk
1 tbsp butter
½ sugar
½ cup molasses
1 large egg or 2 small

Sift the flour, soda, baking powder, salt and spices together and add alternately with sour milk to the creamed butter, sugar, molasses and beaten egg. It may be necessary to add more milk to make the batter like soft whipped cream.

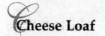

Cheese Loaf

L. C. Kitchen

¼ lb butter
a pinch of salt
¼ lb cheese, grated
3 eggs, beaten
3 cups flour
1 cup milk
2 tsp baking powder

Cream the butter, salt and cheese. Add the eggs, flour and milk gradually. Lastly, add the baking powder. The mixture should be stiff. Bake, and slice when cold.

Bishop's Bread

Mrs. H. E. Wylie

3 eggs, separated
1 cup sugar
1 tsp vanilla
1 cup walnuts, chopped
1 cup raisins
1 cup flour
1 tsp baking powder

Beat the egg whites till stiff, add the yolks and beat again. Sift in the sugar and beat some more. Add vanilla, walnuts, raisins, flour and baking powder. Bake in a shallow tin. When cold, cut in strips and roll in powdered sugar.

Sweet Nut Bread

Mrs. H. E. Wylie

4 cups flour
1 tsp salt
4 tsp baking powder
1¼ cups milk
1 egg
1 cup walnuts, chopped
1 cup sugar

Mix all the ingredients and pour into a loaf tin and let it rise for 30 minutes. Bake slowly for 1 hour.

Walnut and Raisin Bread

Mrs. B. Lucas

2 cups *atta* (wholewheat flour)
1 cup flour
1 cup walnuts and raisins mixed, chopped
1 tsp baking powder
1 tsp soda
2 cups yoghurt
½ cup sugar

Mix all together, beat well and bake.

Nut Bread

Veda B. Harrah

1 egg
1 cup sugar
1 cup milk
3½ cups flour
4 tsp baking powder

1 tsp salt
1 cup walnuts, chopped

Beat the egg. Add the sugar and milk, then the sifted dry ingredients. Beat well and pour into a greased pan. Put into a cool oven. Increase the heat and bake for 30-40 minutes. Note: A splendid recipe.

Walnut Bread
Mrs. Riddle

1 cup flour
1 cup milk
1 cups sugar
1 egg
½ cup walnuts
2 tsp baking powder

Bake for about 1 hour in a moderate oven.

Date Bread

1 cup dates, finely chopped
1 tsp soda
1 cup boiling water
2 tbsp butter, creamed
1½ cups flour
½ cup walnuts
1 egg
a pinch of salt
vanilla
1 cup sugar

Sprinkle soda over the dates. Add the water and the creamed butter. Mix in the remaining ingredients. Bake in a moderate oven for 1 hour.

❦

Raisin and Sour Milk Bread   Mrs. Whitfield

2 cups flour
½ tsp salt
½ tsp soda
1 tsp cream of tartar
2 tbsp sugar
2½ tbsp shortening
½ cup raisins
1 egg

Sift all the dry ingredients together. Rub in the shortening. Add the raisins, beaten egg and enough milk to make a soft dough. Make into a smooth mound and bake in one large or two small pans for ½ an hour in a moderate oven.

❦

Orange Bread

rind of seedless oranges, finely chopped
½ tsp salt
1 cup sugar
2 cups water
2 tbsp shortening, melted
1 egg, well beaten
3 cups flour
3 tsp baking powder

Boil together the orange rind, salt, sugar and 1 cup water for about 15 minutes to make a thin syrup. Cool, and add the remaining water to make 2½ cups. Add the melted shortening and the well-beaten egg. Add the flour sifted with baking powder. Mix thoroughly. Bake in a greased long loaf tin in a moderate oven at 350°F for about 1¼ hours. Makes 1 loaf.

❧

Steamed Brown Bread

Mrs. Stunts

2 cups *atta* (wholewheat flour)
1 cup flour
1 cup *suji* (semolina)
1 tsp soda
1 tsp salt
½ cup sugar, if desired
1 cup raisins
2 cups sour milk
1 cup thick *gur* (molasses)
2 eggs

Mix in all the ingredients and pour in 4 greased tins. Steam for 3 hours steadily.

❧

Brown Bread

2 cups *atta* (wholewheat flour)
1 cup *suji* (semolina)
2 tbsp flour
2 cups sour milk
1 cup *gur* (molasses)

1 tsp soda
1 tsp salt

Mix all the ingredients and place in tins and either steam for 3 hours or bake. The taste will improve if you add 1 cup raisins and 2 egg yolks or one whole egg.

Boston Brown Bread

2 cups white flour
2 cups *atta* (wholewheat flour)
2 tsp baking powder
1 tsp salt
1 cup sweet milk
1 cup golden syrup
1 cup sour milk
1½ tsp soda
1 egg, beaten

Sift together flour, *atta*, baking powder and salt. Pour in the sweet milk mixed with golden syrup and sour milk mixed with soda. Mix in the well-beaten egg. Steam the mixture for 3½ hours in a greased tin.

Bread Dough Cake   J. V. Fleming

2 cups bread dough
(when dough is raised ready for pans)
1 tbsp cinnamon
1 tsp soda
2 cups sugar

1 tsp nutmeg
1 cup butter
1 cup raisins, chopped
4 eggs

Work all the ingredients well together with hand until well mixed and looks like a cake batter. Bake in a slow oven for about 1 hour. It will be very thin but do not add flour as it thickens in baking. This makes one large, or two small cakes, and may be stored for some time. You can also add nuts and candied peel.

Rolls

R. C. Newton

Make sponge as for bread, when it is ready to work out add:

3 eggs, break whole into the sponge

1 cup sugar
1 handful salt
½ cup of cream or ½ cup melted butter (not hot)

Then add 5 cups of flour; knead and set aside to rise to double its size and till it is light. Then divide the dough into small balls about the size of an egg. Dip the top of each dough into some melted butter before placing in the tin. Then let the dough rise again until double its size and light. For long tea rolls, make smaller balls and crowd into a tin so that they rise and are long and light. Bake for 1 hour.

Atta Rolls

E. L. Moody

> 1 cup yeast soaked in 1 cup water
> 4 large potatoes, boiled, finely mashed
> 2 cups flour
> 2 cups warm water

Mix all the ingredients and soak overnight. In the morning, add 2 tbsp butter, 2 tbsp clarified butter, $2/3$ cup sugar and a little salt. Knead well, using 2½ cups *atta* (wholewheat flour) and ½ cup flour. Keep aside in a bowl to rise. Make into rolls and let it rise again. Bake for 20-30 minutes. This recipe can be made with all flour, if desired.

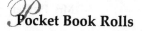

Pocket Book Rolls

E. L. Moody

> 2 cups yeast
> 2 eggs
> ½ cup sugar
> 2 tbsp butter
> ½ cup sweet milk

Mix all the ingredients with 2 cups flour. Keep the mixture in a pan to rise. Roll out ¼″ thick. Cut and grease with butter and fold together. Let it rise and bake in a hot oven for 15-20 minutes.

Date Rolls

2½ cups sugar
1 cup milk
1 tbsp butter
2 cups walnuts

Cook together sugar, milk and butter. When the sugar and milk reach a soft ball stage, add the dates which have been chopped and cooked till melted. Add the butter. Remove from the fire and stir until it begins to set. Mix in the walnuts and work into a roll. Cut in slices.

◆

Muffins

Mrs. Hansen

1 cup flour
2 tsp baking powder
¼ cup sugar
½ tsp salt

Mix the above then add 1 egg, beaten or not, and 1 cup milk. Mix. Add more flour, if necessary, to obtain the same consistency as of cake batter. Raisins added make them nicer.

◆

Corn Muffins

1 egg
6 tbsp sugar
½ cup milk
4 tbsp butter, melted

½ tsp salt
1½ cups flour
1 cup corn *atta* (wholewheat flour)
4 tsp baking powder

Beat the egg, add the sugar, milk and butter. Sift the dry ingredients and add the liquid mixture. Beat thoroughly. Drop the mixture into greased muffin moulds and bake in a moderate oven.

～

Date Muffins

H. H. Brush

2 cups flour
½ tsp salt
½ tsp soda
2 tsp baking powder
3 tbsp sugar
1 egg
1 tbsp shortening
1 cup sour milk
12 dates

One cup of flour may be substituted for one cup of *atta* (wholewheat flour). Mix all the dry ingredients together and stir in the egg, shortening and sour milk beaten together. Put a little batter into the bottom of the muffin tins. Drop a seeded, floured date over this batter and cover each date with more batter. Bake for 20 minutes.

～

Egg Muffins

M. L. Picken

1 egg, beaten very light
1 cup milk
1 cup flour
a pinch of salt

No baking powder needed. Bake in gem pans.

Graham Muffins

3 tbsp flour
½ tsp salt
3 tbsp *atta* (wholewheat flour)
1 tsp baking powder
1 tbsp butter
1 egg

Mix all the ingredients well with enough milk. Bake in a hot oven.

Twin Mountain Muffins

Margaret Mumby

½ cup butter
¼ tsp sugar
1 egg
¾ cup milk
2 cups flour
4 tsp baking powder
¼ tsp salt

Cream the butter and sugar together. Add the egg beaten and mixed with milk Add the flour sifted with baking powder and salt. Bake in hot gem pans for 25 minutes.

Rice Muffins

Mrs. Cornuelle

1 cup milk
½ cup corns
1 tbsp shortening
2 tbsp sugar
1 cup cooked rice
½ cup flour
½ tsp salt
3 tsp baking powder
1 egg

Scald the milk and pour over the corns. And the shortening and sugar. When cold, add the rice and the remaining ingredients and bake for 20 minutes.

Quaker Muffins

Mrs. Strickler

Pour 1 cup of scalded milk over ²/₃ cup of rolled oats and let this stand for 5 minutes. Add the following ingredients and mix:

1 tsp salt
1½ cups flour
4 tsp baking powder
3 tbsp sugar
1 tbsp butter, melted
1 egg

Sour Milk or Buttermilk Scones   C. M. Scott

2 cups flour
1 tsp salt
2 tsp cream of tartar
1 tbsp butter
1 egg
1 tsp soda
1 cup sour milk

Sift the flour, salt and cream of tartar together. Rub the butter
into the flour mixture. Add the beaten egg and sour milk
mixed with soda. Make the dough as soft as possible. Turn it
out into a floured board and pat into shape. Cut out with a
small biscuit cutter and set into a buttered pan. Bake in a
quick oven for about 10 minutes.

Cinnamon Bun

2 tbsp butter
4 tbsp sugar
2 eggs
2 cups flour
3 tsp baking powder
sufficient milk, sugar, cinnamon and currants

Cream the butter and sugar. Add the eggs, flour, baking
powder and milk. Mix and make a dough. Roll out the
dough to ¼" thickness and top with milk, sugar, cinnamon
and currants. Roll up and cut. Bake in a moderate oven.

Scotch Bun
Mrs. Riddle

¼ lb butter
2 oz sugar
3 eggs, beaten
1 cup flour
1 lb currants
1 lb raisins or sultanas
½ tsp powder cloves, if liked
¼ lb peel, cut small
1 nutmeg, grated
1 tbsp cinnamon
½ tsp pepper
½ tsp ginger
2 oz almonds, blanched, chopped

Beat the butter and sugar. Add the eggs, flour and other ingredients. It should be quite dark. Line a large well-buttered tin, fill with the mixture, and bake slowly for 3 hours.

Graham Gems
Mrs. Moody

2 cups *atta* (wholewheat flour)
2 tbsp *ghee* (clarified butter)
1 egg
2 tsp cream of tartar
1 tsp salt
1 tsp soda

Mix all the ingredients and add enough sweet milk to make a batter. Drop into hot greased muffin rings and bake.

Cornmeal Gems

¾ cup corn
1¼ cups flour
1 cup milk (if sour add ½ tsp soda)
2 tbsp sugar
2 tbsp shortening
1 egg, separated

Mix the corn and flour with 4 tsp baking powder and ½ tsp soda. Add the milk, sugar, shortening and well-beaten egg yolk. Mix well. Lastly, fold in the stiffly beaten egg white. Mix well but do not beat the batter. Mix lightly and quickly, the gems then will not be full of holes when done. Bake in a quick hot oven.

❧

Corn Gems
M. L. Picken

½ cup sugar
½ cup butter
2 eggs
2 cups sweet milk
2 cups corn
2 cups flour
3 tsp baking powder

Mix all the ingredients and bake in gem pans.

❧

Cornmeal Griddle Cake

Mrs. E. C. Lochlin

1 cup flour
1 cup cornmeal
1 tbsp baking powder
1 or 2 eggs
1½ tsp salt
2 cups milk

Mix the first three ingredients together. Beat the egg well. Add salt and milk and mix this with the flour mixture. One tbsp molasses may be added to the batter. Bake like any other cake.

Note: 1 tbsp soda and 2 cups sour milk may be used in place of the baking powder and sweet milk.

Quick Coffee Cake

E. L. Moody

1 cup sugar
½ cup butter
3 cups flour
2 tsp baking powder
2 eggs
1 cup milk

Pour the batter in a pan and sprinkle with sugar, cinnamon and a little butter. Bake. This cake is usually served with coffee.

 **Coffee Cake**   E. L. Moody

1 cup strong coffee
1 tsp soda
1 cup molasses
1 cup raisins
1 cup sugar
1 cup citron
4 tbsp butter
1 cup carrots, ground
4 cups flour
2 eggs

You can use ½ cup raisins and ½ cup nuts with a little cinnamon and sugar on top.

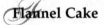

 **Flannel Cake**   E. L. Moody

1 egg
1 cup flour
1 tsp cream of tartar
a pinch of salt
½ tsp soda

Mix all the ingredients and add enough sweet milk to make a very thin batter. Fry in a greased pan and serve with hot syrup.

Beaten Biscuits

E. L. Moody

1 qt flour
1 tsp salt
½ cup lard
½ pt milk and water mixed

Mix the flour, salt and lard together. Moisten to a stiff dough and beat for 30 minutes or more. Bake for 20 minutes in a hot oven.

—❧—

Hot Biscuits

Mrs. Nugent

2 cups flour
1 tsp soda
1 tsp cream of tartar
1 tsp salt
1½ tbsp butter

Mix all the ingredients and make a rather stiff dough. Turn out on a slightly floured board and knead lightly for 2-3 minutes. Roll out lightly to about 1½" thick and cut with a biscuit cutter. Place them well apart on a buttered pan. Prick with a fork and bake in the oven for about 20 minutes. Remove from the oven and brush the tops with sweet cream or butter.

—❧—

Pop Overs

Mrs. L. B. Rambo

3 eggs
2 cups milk
½ tsp salt
2 cups flour

Grease the gem pans or small earthen cups and keep in the oven to get well heated. Beat the eggs, without separating, until very light. Add the milk and salt. Pour this mixture gradually in the flour, stirring all the time. Do not add too quickly or the batter will become so thin that it cannot be beaten smooth. Any little lumps that remain may be strained out with a sieve. Take the hot gem pans out from the oven, quickly fill them half with the batter and put them back to bake for about 25 minutes. They should be brown when done, and should swell 4 times their original bulk.

Waffles

F. W. Ross

1¾ cups flour
3 tsp baking powder
½ tsp salt
1 cup milk
2 eggs
1 tbsp butter, melted

Mix and sift the dry ingredients. Gradually, add the milk, the well-beaten egg yolks, butter and stiffly-beaten egg whites. Mix thoroughly. Cook on a hot waffle-iron. Serve with maple syrup.

Waffles

E. L. Moody

2 cups flour
2 tsp cream of tartar
1 tsp soda
1 tsp salt
2 cups sweet milk
2 eggs, beaten separately
2 tbsp butter, melted

Sift the flour, cream of tartar, soda and salt together. Add the milk and egg yolks. Then add the butter. Fold in the beaten egg whites. Fry in a waffle-iron. Serve with hot syrup.

Cereal Pancakes

Mrs. M. Fawcett

1 tbsp butter, melted
1 tsp sugar
2 eggs, separated
1 cup cooked cereal (or boiled rice or quaker oats)
1 cup milk (if sour add ½ tsp soda)
1½ cups flour
2 tsp baking powder
1 tbsp salt

Mix the butter and sugar together. Add the egg yolks, cereal mixed in milk, flour mixed with baking powder and salt. Mix well. Lastly, add the stiffly beaten egg whites. Fry in a greased pan and serve with hot syrup.

Dumplings for Two

R. C. Newton

1 cup flour
½ cup milk
2 tsp baking powder
½ tsp salt

Mix all the ingredients well together. Drop by spoonfuls into a thickened gravy and steam covered for 15 minutes.

Note: Very simple and never fails.

Lemon Yeast

Mrs. Riddle

The juice of 1 large, or 2 small lemons
2 tbsp flour
2 tbsp sugar
2 cups hot water

Mix all the ingredients well. Store the mixture in a bottle and cork tightly. Shake well and allow it to stand for 24 hours to ferment before use.

Dry Yeast

1 cup of hops in a thin bag
2 medium-sized potatoes
finely chopped with the skin

Boil together until well done, strain through a sieve and add ½ tbsp ginger and 1 tbsp sugar.

Jams and Jellies

Lift up the corners of your mouth,
This is the time to smile.
The wind is blowing 'from the South'
So let's be glad awhile.

Marmalade

Mrs. H. E. Wylie

3 oranges, juice and rind, finely cut
2 lemons, juice and rind of ½ a lemon

Weigh all. To every pound of fruit, add 6 cups water. Cook for 20 minutes and let it stand all night. To every pound of fruit, add 3½ lb sugar. Cook for 40 minutes. This quantity of fruit will make about 6 cups of marmalade.

Rhubarb Marmalade

Miss Drummond

4 lb rhubarb
4 lemons, juice and rind
6 lb sugar
¾ cup walnuts

Mix the first 3 ingredients and cook very carefully for a few minutes, stirring all the while till there is some juice formed. Cook for 15 minutes more. Add the walnuts just before removing from the fire.

Pear Marmalade

12 lb pears, finely chopped
9 lb sugar
1 lb raisins
3 oranges, juice and rind
1 lb shelled walnuts, chopped

Mix all the ingredients and cook till the consistency is right.

Orange Marmalade

6 oranges
2 lemons
4 lb sugar
2 qt water

Slice both the orange and lemon rinds. Pour water over them and let it stand till cold, changing the water several times to remove the bitterness. Cook with the water till tender. Now add the pulp of orange and juice of lemon and sugar. Boil till it becomes syrupy when cold. To 1¼ cups of fruit and juice add, 1 cup sugar (lemon rind can be used in the same way).

Lemon Butter

Mrs. Strickler

1 cup sugar
3 eggs
butter, size of a walnut

Beat all the ingredients together. Add juice and grated rind of 1 large lemon. Cook in a double boiler and stir well until thick.

Lemon Honey made from Vegetable Marrow

2 lb vegetable marrow
2 lb sugar
3 lemons
¼ lb butter

Steam the vegetable marrow and mash it. Add the sugar, lemon juice and grated rind of lemons, and butter. Boil the mixture for ¼ of an hour, or till it thickens, then pour it into jars.

Quince Honey

M. L. Picken

3 pt sugar
2 cups boiling water

Stir the sugar in boiling water and boil till the sugar dissolves. Add 3 large chopped quinces. Boil for 15-20 minutes more.

━━◆━━

Grated Pineapple

Pare the pineapple. Take out the eyes and slice. Put through a meat chopper. To 6 lb prepared fruit and juice, take 3 lb sugar and 3 pt of water and boil together for 3 minutes. Then add the fruit and juice and boil for 10 minutes. Seal immediately.

━━◆━━

Blackberry Jelly

Cover the blackberries with water and boil. Strain out the juice. To 3 parts of juice use 2 parts sugar. Boil rapidly till it drops thickly from the side of the spoon. Put a silver spoon in each glass to prevent the glass from breaking, and pour in the jelly.

Guava juice may be used in the same way to make Guava Jelly. Add lemon juice, if desired.

Guava and Roselle Marmalade

A. B. Cowdry

3 large guavas
2 qt fleshy parts of roselles
3 qt water
sugar

Put the guavas, unpeeled, through a food chopper and then boil with the roselles mashing and stirring till soft. Drain in a coarse jelly bag, or better still put through a fine perforated fruit press. Boil the juice for 20 minutes. Add equal measure of sugar and boil for 5 minutes.

Guava Cheese

J. V. Fleming

6 seers guava pulp
5 seers sugar
1¼ *pao* lemon juice
½ *pao ghee* (clarified butter)

Mix all the ingredients and a little ground cinnamon and cloves, if desired. Cook till very thick so that it will set when cold.

Guava Jam

Peel and slice the ripe guavas and cover the fruit with water. Cook till tender. Cool and rub through a cloth to remove the seeds and to make it fine. Roselle or lemon juice may be added, if desired. Then to 3 parts of fruit use 2 parts sugar. Boil to the consistency of apple-butter, stirring with a wooden spoon.

Plum Jam

Select the plums of a tart variety. Wash the fruit and drain. To each pound of fruit, add ¾ lb sugar and 1 cup water. Boil the plums in water for 10-15 minutes or till the skins are tender. Add the sugar and stir while boiling until the jelly stage is reached. Pour the mixture into hot sterilised jars and seal.

Pickles and Relishes

THE CARROT

Here's to the aristocrat, Carrot,
Pure gold from his heart to his skin
His foes abuse him most roundly,
But his friends just take him right in.

Green Tomato Pickle

R. C. Newton

4 seers green tomatoes, sliced
4 onions, sliced
1 cup salt
4 green peppers, finely chopped
½ oz cloves
½ oz allspice
½ lb brown sugar
½ cup brown mustard seeds

Arrange alternate layers of tomatoes, onions and salt and let this stand overnight. In the morning, wash the vegetables to drain off the salt. Put the mixture in a pan, add the remaining ingredients and pour enough vinegar to cover the mixture. Let the mixture gradually come to a boil. Boil for ½ an hour. Then seal.

Bean Pickle

1 peck butter-beans

Boil the butter-beans in salt water. Then in a separate pan, boil together 3 lb white sugar, 3 pt vinegar, ½ cup mustard, 1 cup flour, 2 tbsp celery seed and 1 tbsp turmeric powder. Pour the mixture over the butter-beans and let it come to a boil. Store in a bottle.

Sliced Cucumber Pickle　　　　E. L. Moody

1 doz cucumbers, sliced
salt
½ cup sugar
3 onions, sliced
2 tsp each white pepper, mustard, ginger
½ pt vinegar
½ stick cinnamon

Sprinkle some salt over the cucumbers and let it stand for 4 hours. Mix all the ingredients and boil for 15 minutes.

Sweet Sliced Pickle

1 gal cucumbers, peeled, sliced
3 medium-sized onions, finely chopped
or 4 sweet green peppers, if available, finely chopped

Soak these for 4 hours, or overnight in salt water. Then scald in the following vinegar mixture:

1½ to 2 qt mild vinegar
5 cups sugar
a pinch of cloves
¾ tsp cinnamon
a dash of paprika
1 tbsp curry powder
1 tbsp celery seed

Scald and cook all the ingredients till the mixture is clear (about ½ hour). The cooking should take place fairly quickly so that the pickles do not soften, but at the same time cook at a simmering boil. Store them in hot sterile jars and seal.

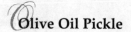# Olive Oil Pickle

Mrs. B. M. Mow

1 gal cucumbers, cut in pieces.
2 cups brown sugar
2 tbsp each celery seed
white mustard seed
olive oil
1 tsp turmeric powder

Soak the cucumber in salt water overnight. Add the vinegar to taste. Boil the mixture with the other ingredients for a while, and store in a jar.

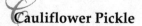# Cauliflower Pickle

Mrs. Donald

½ cauliflower
1½ qt green tomatoes
1 qt onions
2 heads celery
1½ qt cucumbers
2 small green peppers, finely chopped

Soak each vegetable except green peppers separately in salt water overnight. Next morning, combine all the vegetables and cook in the same brine. Remove from the fire and strain. Pour in a dish and chop finely.

Mustard Pickle

J. V. Fleming

> 2 cauliflowers
> 2 qt green tomatoes
> 2 doz small cucumbers
> ½ oz carrots
> 1 qt small onions

Slice the vegetables. Put them in a moderately strong brine and let them stand overnight. Then cook and scald, but do not boil.

Take 3 qt vinegar, ½ oz turmeric, ½ lb mustard, 3½ oz flour and 2 cups sugar and cook till the mixture thickens. Pour this mixture while still boiling over the vegetables. Stir well and when cold store them in bottles.

Mixed Pickle

> 2 qt green tomatoes
> 12 small cucumbers
> 3 red peppers
> 1 cauliflower
> 2 bunches celery
> 1 pt small onions
> 2 qt string beans
> ¼ lb mustard seeds
> 2 oz turmeric powder

Make a syrup of equal parts of sugar and vinegar. Prepare the vegetables and cut them in small pieces. Cover with salt and let them stand overnight and drain. Bring the sugar and vinegar mixture to a good boil. Add the spices and the well-drained vegetables. Cook till the vegetables are tender then fill into jars and seal. Do not use too much salt.

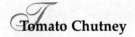

Tomato Chutney

Mrs. M. Fawcett

8 lb tomatoes
8 oz ginger
vinegar
4 lb sugar
2 lb raisins
8 oz salt

If you wish the chutney to be hot, add chillies. Grind the ginger to a thin paste with vinegar. Add the remaining ingredients and cook to the consistency of jam. Stir continuously as it sticks and burns easily. To test if done, put a tiny bit in a saucer. Place the saucer in a pan of cold water. If done (when cool) it will drop thick from the spoon.

❧

Sweet Mango Chutney

Mrs. Core

1 seer green mangoes, sliced
1 seer sugar boiled in 2 cups water
2 *chattaks* garlic
2 *chattaks* ginger
½ seer raisins
2 *chattaks* white mustard seeds
½ bottle vinegar

Stew the mango slowly in sugar syrup and when half done add the other ingredients and simmer to a good consistency for sweet pickle.

Chilli Sauce

Mrs. Davidson

1 peck ripe tomatoes
6 large onions
6 tbsp sugar
4 tbsp salt
chillies to taste

Chop the tomatoes and onions. Add 3 cups vinegar and 3 cups water and bring the mixture to a boil. Add the remaining ingredients, 1 tbsp celery seed, cloves, cinnamon and black pepper powder to taste. Boil till thick (about 3 hours).

Dressing
1½ qt vinegar
1 cup sugar
1 cup flour
½ oz turmeric powder
½ cup mustard
2 eggs, well beaten
butter, size of a walnut

Cook all the ingredients together. Pour the dressing over the pickle. Stir well and boil the entire mixture for a few minutes then bottle.

Tomato Sauce

3 seers tomatoes, cooked, strained
3 tbsp salt
2 garlic cloves
vinegar
3 or 4 small pieces of ginger, sliced

3 cups sugar
5 red pepper

Mix all the ingredients and bring it to a boil. Store in a bottle.

Horseradish Sauce

½ bot horseradish
$^1/_3$ cup water
½ cup sugar
½ cup vinegar
½ tsp mustard
1 cup cream

Soak the horseradish in water and add sugar, vinegar, mustard and cream. Mix well.

Cucumber Relish   Mrs. D. O. Cunningham

1 doz large cucumbers, peeled, cut in thin slices
3 large onions, sliced
1 pt vinegar
1 tsp ground ginger
1 cup sugar
1 stick cinnamon
1 tsp black peppercorns
a few cloves
a little turmeric powder, if desired
1 tsp mustard seeds

Sprinkle some salt over the cucumbers and onions. Let this mixture stand for 4 hours. Add the remaining ingredients and cook for 15 minutes and seal.

Piccalilly

F. W. Ross

Chop 1 peck green tomatoes and 8 onions. Add 1 cup salt, mix well and let it stand overnight. In morning, drain thoroughly and add 2 qt vinegar, 1 lb sugar, ½ lb white mustard seeds, 2 tbsp ground black pepper, 2 tbsp ground cinnamon, 1 tbsp ground ginger, 1 tbsp whole allspice, 1 tbsp cloves and ½ tsp ground cayenne pepper.

Boil all the ingredients together for 15 minutes or till tender, stirring often to prevent scorching.

Watermelon Preserves

E. L. Moody

Peel and cut the watermelon rind in chunks, leaving a little of the red. Cook till tender in a small amount of water. Then to 6 cups of the fruit and juice use 4 cups of sugar. Cut several slices of fresh lemon in and boil until the syrup is thick as desired.

Tamarind Preserves

Remove the hulls from the ripe tamarinds and cook it in water. Cool and strain through a cloth. Use equal parts of sugar and fruit, even more may be required as tamarinds are very sour.

—◆—

Tomato Preserves
E. L. Moody

Scald and peel the ripe tomatoes, yellow or red. Cut in pieces and remove the seeds. Drain. To 3 parts tomato use 2 parts sugar. Put the sugar over the fruit and let it stand overnight. Boil till the juice is syrupy. Flavour with slices of lemon cooked with the mixture or sliced green ginger.

—◆—

Tomato Preserves
Boston Cookbook

1 lb tomatoes
1 lb sugar
2 oz ginger root
2 lemons

Remove the skins from the tomatoes. Add the sugar, cover and let it stand overnight. Pour off the syrup and boil the tomato pulp until quite thick. Skim, then add the ginger root and lemons, sliced. Cook slowly, stirring continuously.

—◆—

Household Hints

1. Make your own baking powder by adding 1 tsp cream of tartar to ½ tsp soda.

2. Use noodles with cheese in place of macaroni.

3. To kill the mutton taste in mutton, add 2 peeled apples.

4. In place of whipped cream, beat 2 egg whites stiffly, add a little sugar and 2 or 3 tbsp cream. Stir the cream in gently. This is good for Gelatin Pudding.

5. Mix the chapatti dough with milk instead of water. It makes them softer.

6. Use the water in which the vegetables have been cooked for soup instead of plain water. Also rice water is good.

7. In the hills, use less sugar in baking.

8. To keep diced apples white, put them in a bowl of water with a little vinegar.

9. Substitute birthday candle holders by sticking a candle into a marshmallow, or use a wire holder with a paper or natural flower.

10. Ornamental cookies are nice to hang on a Christmas tree.

Vitamins

Vitamins are organic substances present in small amounts in all foods. They carry out the vital functions of the body. Although they are needed in small amounts, they are essential for health and the well being of the body.

Vitamin A is needed for the growth and repair of the body. It also prevents the body from infectious diseases.

Foods rich in vitamin A are: cod liver oil, fish oil, fat fish, egg yolk, clarified butter, liver, kidney, mutton, animal fats, milk, spinach, lettuce, watercress, celery leaves, cabbage, turnip tops, beetroot tops, radish tops and bamboo tops.

Vitamin B is needed to keep the brain, nerves, heart, liver, digestive glands, kidneys and muscles healthy and strong including those of the bowels.

Foods rich in vitamin B are: yeast, egg, liver, tomato, celery, radish tops and watercress.

Vitamin C deficiency causes scurvy which is characterised by weakness, bleeding gums and defective bone growth. This vitamin is easily destroyed by heat. It is needed by the body to keep the blood pure; to help the other vitamins in building, especially the bones and teeth; to keep the bowel movement healthy and resist any body infection.

Foods rich in vitamin C are: fresh raw cabbage, spinach, fresh lemon and orange juice, tomatoes and tomato juice.

Vitamin D is required for bone growth and calcium metabolism. Lack of it leads to rickets and osteomalacia (pain in the bones). This plays an important role in the absorption of dietary calcium from the intestines and its deposition in bone. Gross deformities of bone may, therefore, result if enough vitamin D is not available to the body.

Foods rich in vitamin D are: cod liver oil, milk, clarified butter and egg yolk.